PROPHESY
FROM A
Pure
STREAM

Releasing the Flow of the Spirit
Through the Prophetic Word of God

TINA McCORKLE

LIFEWISE BOOKS

PROPHESY FROM A PURE STREAM
Releasing the Flow of the Spirit Through the Prophetic Word of God

All verses quoted are from NIV unless otherwise noted.

Scriptures marked KJV are taken from the KING JAMES VERSION (KJV): KING JAMES VERSION, public domain.

THE HOLY BIBLE, NEW INTERNATIONAL VERSION®, NIV® Copyright © 1973, 1978, 1984, 2011 by Biblica, Inc.® Used by permission. All rights reserved worldwide.

Published by:

⚙ LIFEWISE BOOKS

PO BOX 1072
Pinehurst, TX 77362
LifeWiseBooks.com

To contact the author: tinamccorkle.com
ISBN (Print): 978-1-952247-28-6
ISBN (Ebook): 978-1-952247-29-3

ACKNOWLEDGEMENTS

I am so very grateful for all the people that have loved me and walked beside me through thick and thin as I have been walking this journey with Jesus.

First, I want to thank my mom for being my number one cheerleader. Her encouragement over the years has kept me going when I felt like giving up.

I want to thank my husband Steve McCorkle for standing for our marriage and believing in the gifts and callings in my life. My husband believes in teamwork; and as husband and wife, he has released me to go wherever the Lord calls.

To my four children: Nathan, Michael, Alicia and Christy who have been sources of joy and challenge over the years, and who now stand with me as they bless me. Over time they have become my dearest friends.

CONTENTS

FOREWORD

The first time I heard Tina McCorkle speak was at the 2014 Woman's Passion & Purpose Conference in Olympia, WA. I saw a dynamic woman of God called to empower the Body of Christ for such a time as this. Tina's passion and the way she communicates with wisdom from her heart, stirs a desire for more of God. Our friendship has grown since then as we have ministered together, mentored others, and shared many rich times in prayer.

As Aurora Worldwide's lead facilitator and teacher since 2010, I've ministered to many through personal inner-healing prayer sessions, teaching classes/workshops, and speaking at conferences and church groups. I am often on the lookout for good supportive resources that help strengthen the ability to hear God's voice and remove the hinderances that block them. *Prophesy from a Pure Stream - Releasing the Flow of the Spirit Through the Prophetic Word of God* is such a resource. It offers keys, encouragement, and examples of what is needed to hear from God and be encouraged from His inspiration personally.

Tina's vivid writing style is both engaging and revelatory. You will have immediate gain. She lays out the cleansing filters as means to clear away what disconnects us from God. As I dove into the book, God was creating in me a clean heart and renewing a steadfast spirit within me. (Psalm 51:10) Tina's scriptural teaching, together with stories from her rich life experiences, construct a solid foundation in God's ways of freeing and cleansing us from the interferences of this world.

I recognize her seasoned discernment and loving understanding of God's goodness that propels us to know and experience Him more. The significant prayer exercises she includes at the end of each chapter provide immediate opportunities to apply what washes the heart anew. I was inspired to apply the principles and pray the prayers she outlines. Her book is a valuable tool that empowers and equips readers to purify the streams of their hearts to hear God purely. I highly recommend it!

This book teaches how to flow from a pure stream to hear God's heart. I believe every intercessor, worship leader, prophetic minister, and anyone who wants to be closer to God, will find *Prophesy from a Pure Stream* a compelling read. They will greatly benefit, be renewed, and aligned in the pure streams of His Spirit.

I pray as you read this book, you will experience God's cleansing waterfall of life and truth washing over you. Not only that, may you be inspired to rise up empowered, to be a pure stream of His life that the world greatly needs.

Elizabeth RoBless-Johnson
Founder & President of Aurora Worldwide Ministries
Healing and Equipping for the Heart & Soul
auroraworldwide.org

INTRODUCTION

This book's journey began with a vision a few years ago. I was in the middle of a worship service when it played out before me. I saw soldiers moving all over an area of land. Some were climbing up a huge mountain and others were in the valley. Many looked battle-worn, like they had been in the fight for some time. Some had uniforms, tattered and torn, covered in mud. Others wore the same uniform but newer looking and clean.

I asked the Lord, *"What does this vision mean?"*

The Lord began to explain that the soldiers represented many of God's prophets. Some were seasoned and mature. Others were just learning how to hear God's voice.

The ones covered in mud had been in the trenches a while. The regional mud had clung to their clothing, but they were unaware. So, they kept fighting instead of pulling back to regroup, assess and clean up. What they needed was rest physically and spiritually. But they felt so duty bound, they continued on.

Those that had cleaner uniforms were a mixture of new believers that were learning to hear God's voice and learning to battle as well as those who, by experience, had learned the importance of taking time away to refuel themselves, recalibrate and clean up in the presence of the Lord.

The Lord then began to speak to me about His desire for His prophets to speak from a pure stream. To be clear, these prophets are those who hear the Lord and share what they hear with the Body. They train and equip. The Lord spoke to me in the vision that many of His children had not slowed down enough to get cleaned up. Some of the mud was simply from battles they had fought and had nothing to do with personal sin. The regional mud did affect whether they were able to hear God clearly because it affected the words that were being released. Many words were not fully coming to pass as spoken or expected as a result of not slowing down and getting their minds renewed.

I asked the Lord about this. *"What is to be done, Lord? If being in the battle of life makes you muddy, what are we to do?"*

He then began to show me keys. They were keys to flowing in a pure stream. These keys enabled the ones listening to God to receive confidence. It was a confidence that they are rightly connected to him and therefore hearing correctly.

The Lord desires for all His children to hear His voice and to flow in a pure stream. He wants all His prophets to bring forth pure words of encouragement to the Body of Christ through prophecies that are fulfilled. He longs to speak to us and wants us to hear Him clearly.

Come with me on a journey of discovery toward the place called the pure stream.

Section One

KEYS TO A PURE STREAM

Chapter One
BECOMING A WORSHIPER

Battles and Bumps in the Night

My husband and I had just bought our first home. We were so excited as we packed up our belongings. There we were with our first-born son, who was two years old at the time, and with another son on the way. We were your typical first-time homebuyers, full of excitement and ready for the next chapter of our lives. This home, family, and marriage thing was feeling "real."

We had been in the home only a short while, when I began to hear unusual sounds while no one else was there except my son. I had been told that sounds could bleed out of your television cable line, so I called the cable guy and they confirmed. Yes, that does happen. The cable company sent a service repair man out to investigate. Sure enough, he said the cable needed replacing and the change should take care of the problem.

But now instead of hearing random sounds such as a piano playing, I could feel the presence of a demonic spirit. This went on for several years as I would lay down in my room after putting the children to bed. By this time, I had three children, two sons and one daughter. Often, as I would drift off to sleep, I would feel someone patting the end of my bed. I would wake up, but no one was there. I would drift back to sleep only to have it happen again.

Soon it began to affect my children. My sons at five and three years of age both came to me terrified, saying they saw something in the nursery bedroom. My oldest said the spirit wanted to kill him and the younger son said he felt an angel was there as well.

Both children needed consoling. I prayed for them and commanded the spirit of fear off them and out of the house. I processsed with them the best I knew how. I wanted them to know that our God is greater, that even if the enemy wanted to scare them, God would scare the enemy.

I had many people, including close friends and pastors from our local church, come and pray over our home, but the oppression would not lift. During this time, my husband and I were having serious marital problems, too. It was a time that some call the dark night of the soul. I asked the Lord, *"Where are You?"*

The nightly reports to my husband about the demonic activity only made matters worse. My husband thought something was wrong with me. He doubted my mental stability, partially because he slept right through it. He was never harassed at night. My children reported seeing scary eyes or hearing noises on the steps but not my husband. He saw nothing and heard nothing. Needless to say, we were not operating as a one-flesh team taking the enemy out as we should have been.

One hot summer night, we decided to bring down a couple of the mattresses, lay them out on the floor of the basement, and sleep as a family on one giant bed. By this time, we had four children, two sons and two daughters. That night while trying to sleep, I kept feeling something flying over me. It pressed down on me, and then lifted up and off, only to do it again.

I was done. I woke my husband and said, *"You are getting up now and we are praying together about this."* I expressed being over it and that we would move if nothing changed. He got up very grumpy muttering *"I just cannot believe this."* As we sat in the living room, my husband began to pray. He said something like, *"God if this is real as my wife says, I need you to show me."*

Bang! A loud noise came from the nursery bedroom upstairs. My husband looked at me with wide eyes. We both realized the crib had been slammed against the wall and no one was upstairs.

Our children were all fast asleep in the basement. My husband stood up and started upstairs. The hair on his arm stood up, he looked at me and said, *"Something evil is up there."* I began to pray in the Spirit as my husband went upstairs to command it out of the house in the name of Jesus.

My husband came downstairs and apologized to me for not believing me or standing with me all these years. He promised to believe me the next time I gave him spiritual information, whether good or bad. This was a great beginning for our marriage. My husband began to understand that I have the gift of a seer, which is a way to receive information from the Lord. Like Jeremiah and other prophets in the Bible, God shows seers pictures or visions as another means to speak to them. Seers usually have the gift of discerning of spirits and may see angels and demons. Prior to this, he simply did not understand where I was coming from, and therefore discredited my insights.

He also learned that he could trust me, his wife. This was a great victory. I learned first-hand that promises of God are "Yes" and "Amen." But remember, life is not a drive through window at a burger joint. Changes take time. Answers to prayers also take time especially when they involve the will of another person. People prematurely give up on marriages, other relationships, or assigned tasks. Some things simply take time. We are human beings, not microwaves. Be patient, stand on God's promises and wait for the vision to come to pass.

Now, back to my story. This was the beginning for our one flesh ministry and marriage, but the house was still not fully cleansed. It had only been quiet for a while. One morning, after having a rough night of the usual tapping on the bed and a creepy feeling in my room, I went into the baby nursery to pray.

I began by commanding the demons to leave and rebuking them as various preachers had taught me, but this time, the Lord stopped me. I heard the voice of the Lord so clearly. He said, *"Tina, the enemy would wear you out. Begin to praise me. Get the Psalms and begin to read them out loud. Read them and praise me. Keep praising me. Sing and shout out loud who I am, and you will see the enemy leave."*

Oh, my goodness. Why didn't I get this before? Why did all the teaching I had come across tell me to rebuke the enemy in Jesus' name as the only method of cleansing? I began to prophesy from a pure stream. I challenge you to desire the ability to stop your plan of action and listen to His plan of action. Lay down your previous plans and old habits of doing things to receive something new and fresh from Him. This instruction from God was transforming.

First, I was transformed as I praised Him. Then the atmosphere in my home was transformed as the presence of Jesus filled the room. When you praise the Lord with intentionality, knowing this is your God given weapon, watch out. The enemy will flee. I am telling you this brought the breakthrough. God bless all the people who prayed through my home. I am grateful. I may never know how their prayers held the enemy back. However, the victory was won with the power of praise.

I love to read 2 Chronicles 20 any time I feel overwhelmed. Each time I read the chapter, I marvel at the power of praise and worship as a weapon. Angels are released as we proclaim who God is. This knowledge has led me into a lifestyle of worship.

> *Psalm 149:1-9 "Praise the LORD. Sing to the LORD a new song, his praise in the assembly of his faithful people. Let Israel rejoice in their Maker; let the people of Zion be glad in their King. Let them praise his name with dancing and make music to him with timbrel and harp.*
>
> *For the LORD takes delight in his people; he crowns the humble with victory. Let his faithful people rejoice in this honor and sing for joy on their beds. May the praise of God be in their mouths and a double-edged sword in their hands, to inflict vengeance on the nations and punishment on the peoples, to bind their kings with fetters, their nobles with shackles of iron, to carry out the sentence written against them— this is the glory of all his faithful people. Praise the LORD."*

Adoration

Adoration comes from your heart, when your mind is focused on something or someone in whom you see traits of beauty or character that you admire or love. We can admire and adore many things. When we can step into that place of adoration of God, it's like none other. We become fully absorbed with who He is. When we adore the Lord, it is not just about how special He is or what He has done for us. It is a 'feeling' of truly loving Him. Our hearts are tugged and drawn to our magnificent God. We cannot get enough of Him. We drink Him in. It's like looking at a spectacular view of the snow-covered mountains with a blanket of white everywhere as far as the eye can see. It takes our breath away. When adoration toward the Lord fills our hearts, we are drawn into Him, thus, preparing the way for true worship to take place.

I struggled with mild depression as a young woman. I would experience what some call the blues. I recall the first couple of years after rededicating my life to Jesus, fighting to pull out of thoughts of despair. I felt lonely. Before walking with the Lord, I entertained myself by going out with friends to various parties. But when I rededicated my life to the Lord, I wanted to please Him. I learned by reading my Bible that getting drunk with alcohol was not on God's top five things that pleased him. In fact, it was on His "not to do" list, if there is such a thing.

I talked with my mom about this and other older women who encouraged me to get to church, participate in the singles group or college and career group. So, I did. I went to a variety of gatherings hoping to make friends with the Christian young people.

Even there, I felt left out somehow, like I didn't truly belong. I wondered how I would live the rest of my life so depressed. During this time period, I was renting a travel trailer 8 feet wide and 40 feet long from my grandparents. In this small but quaint space, I learned the art of shifting my focus from myself, onto God. I later learned from scriptures that what I was experiencing was a spirit of heaviness. While reading the Bible, I saw that God will give us a divine exchange. When we give Him the spirit of heaviness, He gives us a garment of praise.

Isaiah 61:3 "…and provide for those who grieve in Zion— to bestow on them a crown of beauty instead of ashes, the oil of joy instead of mourning, and a garment of praise instead of a spirit of despair. They will be called oaks of righteousness, a planting of the Lord for the display of his splendor."

I began to praise the Lord in that little trailer, singing as loud as my heart was content to do. I would adore the Lord and sing in my prayer language. Guess what? The depression lifted right off me as tears rolled down my cheeks for joy. It was the joy of seeing in that moment how beautiful my God was. My eyes were no longer on myself. They were on my beautiful God. There is an old hymn that I appreciate to this day. It goes, *"Turn your eyes upon Jesus, look full in his wonderful face, and the things of the earth will grow strangely dim, in the light of his glory and grace."* [1]

Think of the goodness and kindness of God. When you do, all despair will leave you in the light of His glory. The meditation of His goodness cannot dwell together with sorrows. Even if your circumstances are so very hard, they will not crush you.

Ephesians 2:6 "And God raised us up with Christ and seated us with him in the heavenly realms in Christ Jesus."

We are not seated in lower places of helplessness, but rather we are seated with Christ in heavenly ones.

No one ever said the Christian journey would be an easy one. Jesus made that clear.

John 16:33 "I have told you these things, so that in me you may have peace. In this world you will have trouble. But take heart! I have overcome the world."

Learning to live in the place of His presence takes time to cultivate. We can practice becoming aware of His presence. Personally, I cannot imagine life without the constant presence of my loving God.

I was so hungry for more of God, I went on a pilgrimage of sorts with three of my friends to the International House of Prayer in Kansas City. The day we arrived, we were looking forward to the 24-hour prayer and worship room. I will never forget how we all were looking around, soaking up everything we could. We chose to sit in the back row to observe, because we did not know what to expect.

While sitting in the back and soaking in the atmosphere of God's weighty presence, I began to thank Him for the moment, praise Him for His goodness, and adore Him for His brilliant beauty. My arms became glued to my seat. I could not move. My whole body was saturated in the presence of the Lord. Tears began to stream down my face as I began to see visions full of outstanding brilliance and color. I saw planets and stars; it was as if I was looking at another galaxy. I was in awe. I had never before experienced such visions.

In one of the visions I saw several dancers worshiping the Lord. As they gracefully dipped and flowed, I saw breakthrough begin to happen. What looked like an ice wall began to crack during the dance until it was completely shattered. Once it was broken, the wind of God flowed freely all around.

I was undone. In the natural, no one was dancing; but the vision from God brought further revelation of the power of dance in worship. If I had ever doubted my desire to dance before the Lord, the doubt was absolutely crushed as I watched this beautiful display of God's power for breakthrough.

We know that David danced in his undergarments before the Ark of the Lord. It was a victory dance full of praise and thanksgiving. As Michal, his wife, watched on in pure disgust, David danced on saying, *"I will become even more undignified than this"* (see 2 Samuel 6:21-22). David put God first and his reputation second.

It is important for us to ask ourselves, *"Am I willing to be more undignified as David was?"* There is so much more for us in God. We should remember to be careful not to limit either Him or ourselves. If breakthroughs to victory can come through dance, then let's dance. Since the Word of God is full of promises, let's act as if these promises are real. God has given us many keys from the Word to benefit us. They are keys that will lead to our success on this earth.

Get your praise on, then move into adoring Him for all that He is and all that He will do. You will feel better and hear His voice much clearer.

Worship

When I first began to learn about worshiping God, I was inspired by Mary, the mother of Jesus. In Luke 1:35-38, we read that Mary had an encounter with the Angel of the Lord. He told her she would be the mother of the Son of God. Mary asked how it would happen because she was a virgin.

The angel explained that the Holy Spirit would come on her, the power of the Most High would overshadow her and she would conceive a child. Mary responded, *"I am the Lord's servant... May your word to me be fulfilled.' Then the angel left her."* [2] Her words speak of complete surrender and trust.

We read about Elizabeth and her miracle of conceiving a child in her old age. This child was also to be a player in the grand scheme of things, the one who would prepare the way for the Lord. His name would be John. We know him as John the Baptist. Mary went to visit with her relative, Elizabeth. I believe this was to get out from under the scrutiny of people in her hometown. Mary, who was betrothed to Joseph, may have been concerned with her present condition. She was a virgin and yet expecting a child. How would she ever explain that?

When Elizabeth heard Mary's greeting, she was filled with the Holy Spirit and her child who would be called John leapt in her womb. Elizabeth began to exalt the Lord and proclaim Mary as the mother of her Lord. She could have only known this by the Holy Spirit.

Mary begins to sing and worship the Lord in Luke 1:46-55:

> *"And Mary said, 'My soul glorifies the Lord and my spirit rejoices in God my Savior, for he has been mindful of the humble state of his servant. From now on all generations will call me blessed, for the Mighty One has done great things for me - holy is his name. His mercy extends to those who fear him, from generation to generation.*
>
> *He has performed mighty deeds with his arm; he has scattered those who are proud in their inmost thoughts He has brought down rulers from their thrones, but has lifted up the humble. He has filled the hungry with good things but has sent the rich away empty. He has helped his servant Israel, remembering to be merciful to Abraham and his descendants forever, just as he promised our ancestors."*

Worship is the grateful response of our heart to our beautiful God. It is a place of deep surrender. Mary was carried away by the Holy Spirit as she praised Him, thanked Him and worshiped Him. I believe this is a natural flow from spirit to Spirit as we exalt His holy name.

Psalm 42 was written by Makil, a descendant of the sons of Korah. Korah was a Levite who rebelled against the Lord when Moses was leading the Hebrews in the wilderness. There was a great calling on this man and his family; but because of their rebellion, the earth swallowed them up. They were not only in rebellion but leading others to follow suit. Thankfully, that wasn't the end of the story.

We see God's redemptive plan unfold. Later, a descendant of Korah, wrote to the Lord in worshipful song and prayer.

> *Psalm 42:7 "Deep calls to deep in the roar of your waterfalls; all your waves and breakers have swept over me."*

You can hear the longing in this Psalm for more of God. This is a cry for a place where hearts connect. When worship of God comes from a place of longing and hunger to be with Him, you will experience His presence like waves washing over you or diving into deep waters, surround by His presence.

In Ezekiel, we read about the River of Life. I call it this because it says where the river flows, everything will live. This scripture parallels how we often begin in our worship to God. We start out in the shallow waters as we lift our hands and begin to connect with God on a deeper level as we continue to worship. Oh, to dive into the deep places with God.

> *Ezekiel 47:3-6 "As the man went eastward with a measuring line in his hand, he measured off a thousand cubits and then led me through water that was ankle-deep. He measured off another thousand cubits and led me through water that was knee-deep. He measured off another thousand and led me through water that was up to the waist. He measured off another thousand, but now it was a river that I could not cross, because the water had risen and was deep enough to swim in—a river that no one could cross. He asked me, 'Son of man, do you see this?'"*

Jesus said the Father is looking for worshipers who will worship Him in spirit and in truth.[3] We as created beings have a body, mind and spirit. I believe the Father is looking for those who know the truth of who He is and those who allow their spirit man to worship Him, not just through their intellect (mind). Worship from our intellect alone leaves the Father longing for more.[4] God is a relational God. He longs to connect with His children. He delights in our longing to connect with Him.

I discovered years ago the value of getting alone with God. One of my favorite things to do is to go into my bedroom, shut the door, put on worship/soaking music and lay on the floor. You may ask, "Why lay on the floor and not the bed?" On the floor, I am awake and alert. Doing this opens my senses to hear from Him and see pictures or visions as He speaks to me. It connects me in a deeper way as I lay there and worship. The beauty of His presence comes alive in the room and surrounds me. Often, tears roll down my face as we connect once again.

The Wonders of His Glory

When people speak of the glory of God, they are normally speaking of the presence of God; the presence that fills the room. His presence is weighty and tangible. This is not the same as the presence of the Holy Spirit that lives in you when you ask Jesus into your heart; nor the presence that fills you with dunamis power like in Acts chapter 2. In the glory of God, He alone is working and moving.

This is the place where many have seen miracles such as bodies healed when no one prayed for them. Hearts are healed in glory. People can be seen weeping as the glory comes into the room during worship. Hands have dripped with oil from heaven. Visions are seen of heavenly things. Angels are seen or felt in glory.

2 Chronicles 5:11-14 "The priests then withdrew from the Holy Place. All the priests who were there had consecrated themselves, regardless of their divisions. All the Levites who were musicians—Asaph, Heman, Jeduthun and their sons and relatives—stood on the east side of the altar, dressed in fine linen and playing cymbals, harps and lyres. They were accompanied by 120 priests sounding trumpets. The trumpeters and musicians joined in unison to give praise and thanks to the Lord. Accompanied by trumpets, cymbals and other instruments, the singers raised their voices in praise to the Lord and sang:

'He is good; his love endures forever.'

Then the temple of the Lord was filled with the cloud, and the priests could not perform their service because of the cloud, for the glory of the Lord filled the temple of God."

Often people are in a hurry on Sunday mornings when they go to a church service. There is a routine we get used to, sing four songs followed by announcements. Then the pastor preaches His Word followed by lunch afterward.

My husband and I both lead worship. We agree that as we are leading worship, we do not want to move into the message until we have sensed the strong presence of the Lord in the room. We know that the presence of God's glory can feel different for everyone. However, many have shared their experiences in the Glory and their stories are similar. Most people have told me they can physically feel the weighty presence of the Lord. Remember the story I shared earlier about going to International House of Prayer and being glued to my seat? That's the glory I'm talking about. You may not always feel like you are glued to a seat, but you will sense His glorious presence in the room.

After completing a 40-day Daniel fast, I was feeling a little oppressed and most of it had to do with walking through some very difficult circumstances. Walking through hard times in life can be a battle to keep the faith. I reached out to a friend of mine for prayer. We went into my office, sat down and began to thank the Lord. As we were thanking Him and blessing His name, we felt a shift inside of us. We stayed in a place of holy awe of who God is, when suddenly the room filled with the glory of the Lord. It almost took our breath away.

I was glued to my chair and could barely move. It felt as if I was in an airplane going straight up with gravity pressing against me. As I was experiencing this, my friend began to laugh. She explained excitedly that she could smell rose petals. I soon realized an Angel of the Lord was in the room with us. This angel was on assignment to strengthen me for all I was going through and what was to come. How do I know this?

The angel spoke to me. He said, "I am here to strengthen you for what is to come". I did not see the angel with my natural eyes but with my spiritual eyes.

This happened to Daniel after he received a vision. He was weak from a fast and from what he had just witnessed. The Angel of the Lord was with him to strengthen him so he could stand and continue to receive the word of the Lord.

> Daniel 10:17-19 "How can I, your servant, talk with you, my Lord? My strength is gone, and I can hardly breathe.' Again, the one who looked like a man touched me and gave me strength. 'Do not be afraid, you who are highly esteemed,' he said. 'Peace! Be strong now; be strong.' When he spoke to me, I was strengthened and said, 'Speak, my Lord, since you have given me strength.'"

This is exactly what happened to me. After the angel told me he was there to strengthen me for what was to come, I began to receive visions. The visions indicated the great warfare I was about to go through. The visions showed me that with God's help, I would go through the fire and not be burned. Praise God. I thought things were hard when I asked my friend for prayer that day; however, things were about to get a whole lot tougher. I may not have endured what was to come if I had not been strengthened by the angel and soaked in the glorious presence of the Lord.

Hearing the voice of the Lord in glory can be life changing. You cannot help but long for more of Him in a tangible way. God changes hearts. God heals bodies. God longs for souls to be saved from the enemies' destructive ways. It is our God who releases the prophetic word. The Lord's mercy endures forever. Praise Him, adore Him, worship Him and become more aware of the glory of His presence. It is in His presence when we receive prophetic words and visions from the Lord. This is where the pure stream is and comes from.

Activation Prayer:

Heavenly Father, I thank You for all the wonderful truths You have given in Your word. You have given us the keys of praise and worship to silence the enemy. Teach us to praise You with grateful hearts and to learn to cultivate Your presence as we worship You. Bring us to Your pure streams, that we may drink deeply in Your presence. In Jesus' name. Amen.

Chapter Two
PRAYER

Communication

Prayer is the connecting force between you and God. Prayer is powerful. Prayer is our communication with God. Communication is vital in every culture and in every relationship. This is also important in our relationship with God. It is amazing to know that God hears the prayers of His children and, in fact, uses prayer to bring about His will on earth. Our Heavenly Father created this design of communication from the beginning, it was always His intention to respond to our prayers.

> *1 John 5:14 "This is the confidence we have in approaching God: that if we ask anything according to his will, he hears us."*

It is so amazing to think that the God of the Universe listens to us. That He not only listens, as if that's not mind-blowing enough, but that He answers our prayers. Prayerlessness is like trying to turn on a lamp that is not plugged in. Prayer plugs us into the power source. Without prayer, there is no light; however, prayer is more than that. According to the Word of God, He sends angels to do many things for us that we have asked of Him. We are told to be careful, because we never know when we may be entertaining angels unaware.

> *Hebrews 13:2 "Do not forget to show hospitality to strangers, for by so doing some people have shown hospitality to angels without knowing it."*

Why do you think God's angels are here? They are here because the Lord sends them. God knows we need help. Help often comes with angels. I had an encounter such as this scripture describes. Entertaining angels unaware. I would like to share the story with you.

My aunt Gloria spent a great deal of time studying eschatology (end times) and had a book written in novel form from the early 1900's. I don't even remember the title of the book, only that it was gripping to read. Each page I turned had me sitting on the edge of my seat in a dramatic action movie. My aunt told me the book was out of print and it was her only copy, so I had to be very careful to make sure I returned it to her. Because I am a first born by nature and upbringing, the sense of responsibility was always with me in everything I did. Caring for this book was no different.

I kept the book in my car and read it during my lunch break, as well as reading it at home in my free time. When I finished the book, I thought I had placed it in my car so I could return it to her. But the very thing I tried so hard not to do, I did. I lost the book.

I searched high and low for this book and nothing. It was nowhere to be found. I even had my brother take out the seats of my car. Nothing. I went on a three-day water fast. I was determined to do whatever it took to find this book. I definitely communicated with God. Words like, *"Oh, God you have got to help me find this book"* poured out of me.

The last day of my three-day fast as I was driving home from work, I saw a hitchhiker standing by the freeway entrance. The hitchhiker was a young man. Normally, I would never even consider stopping to pick up a hitchhiker, male or female. But I was completely drawn to help him. I silently prayed for God's protection as I pulled over.

We talked as I drove, but nothing profound was said. I mentioned that I lived in Puyallup in my grandparents' trailer, then I asked where he was going.

He said, *"Bonney Lake."*

I replied, *"Okay, I'll take you there."*

He was surprised and said, *"But that will be out of your way."*

I continued driving. I told him it was no problem and that I was glad to be of help. When we got to his destination, he let me know that I could pull the car over near an upcoming driveway that he pointed out. He thanked me for my kindness, closed the door and began to walk away from the car. I looked down at the empty space where the man had been sitting. The missing book was lying there. I quickly looked up and the man was gone. I mean gone. I drove up and down the road with tears of wonder falling down my face. The realization hit me. This man was sent by God to bring me the book. I believe he was an angel.

Yes, God hears our prayers; however, answers don't usually come right away. Sometimes, we must go the extra mile with prayer and fasting. It seems that angels respond to God's children when they fast and pray. When reading the book of Daniel, you see a great example of this. Daniel's fasting and prayer moved Gabriel to bring him the needed revelation in Daniel 9-10. How many times have you possibly entertained angels unaware?

As you think of prayer as your conversation with God, think of this: little babies know how to communicate. Before they know the language of their culture, they use body language and sounds, such as cries and laughter. If a mother or father knows how to respond to their baby, how much more will your Heavenly Father respond to you?

Petitions and Requests

Most Christians have perfected this part of prayer easily. We learn quickly to take our needs to the Lord. Yet the disciples recognized they were possibly missing something in prayer when they asked Jesus to teach them how to pray. Perhaps after watching Jesus often retreat to pray alone, the importance of prayer began to stir their hearts. Perhaps they too hungered for more.

After Jesus was asked the question, Lord teach us to pray, we find his answer in Matthew.

> *Matthew 6:9-13 "This, then, is how you should pray: 'Our Father in heaven, hallowed be your name, your kingdom come, your will be done, on earth as it is in heaven. Give us today our daily bread. And forgive us our debts, as we also have forgiven our debtors. And lead us not into temptation, but deliver us from the evil one.'"*

There is so much meat in this one example of prayer taught by Jesus that this chapter on prayer could be wholly devoted to it, but I will only use the parts that apply to prayer. In the Lord's prayer, we see how Jesus first honors the Father and His name. Jesus then makes a decree and a declaration saying, *"Your kingdom come, your will be done on Earth as it is in Heaven."* [1] Jesus, demonstrates how to ask for your needs with the example *'give us our daily bread.'* Something Jesus also makes clear with this prayer is that we need to be sure we are forgiving others and asking to be forgiven. Finally, we ask God to not lead us into temptation, but deliver us from evil.

The Bible is full of scriptures either role modeling how to make a request to God or exhorting us to make requests to God.

> *Philippians 4:6 "Do not be anxious about anything, but in every situation, by prayer and petition, with thanksgiving, present your requests to God."*

Hannah's story from the Bible is most profound. It tells of a woman bringing her petitions and requests to God, and how God answered those requests. Hannah was married to a man named Elkanah. Hannah could not have children because the Lord had closed her womb. To make matters worse, Elkanah had another wife whose name was Peninnah. Peninnah did have children, so she would torment Hannah and ridicule her because she had children and Hannah did not.

One day, when they had gone into Shiloh to eat and offer sacrifices to the Lord as a family, Hannah got up, went to the temple and began to cry out to God for a son. Eli, the priest, saw her and thought she was drunk because he did not hear her words. He only saw her mouth moving and her body shaking as she wept. After the priest accused her of being drunk, Hannah was able to speak to Eli and convince him that she was not drunk but was just crying out to God.

Eli had a change of heart towards Hannah and began to bless her. He asked the Lord to give her whatever she was asking for. Hannah wanted her womb blessed so she could have children. Hannah left the temple with hope in her heart and the next day worshiped the Lord with her husband. After returning home, Hannah lay with her husband Elkanah and conceived a son. Hannah had told the Lord she would give the son to the Lord to be raised in the temple with Eli, the priest.

The Lord indeed had opened her womb, Hannah was true to her word in giving Samuel to the priest. She regularly visited her son, Samuel, when they returned to Shiloh to offer yearly sacrifices to the Lord (see 1 Samuel 1:1-2:11). Samuel became one of the most respected prophets in Biblical times. As for Hannah, she later had five additional children.

Be specific in your requests to God. Hannah was very specific. She asked for a son and offered to give the son back to God if He would grant her request. I believe that if Hannah were here today, she would say, *"Children of the Lord do not give up. Keep on praying. Keep on asking the Lord for the longing in your heart. Our God is faithful."*

As a young woman trying to find my place in life, I began seeking God for direction. I decided to fast for three days and get alone with God. I felt such restlessness in my soul at the time. If I am honest, I was discontent with my circumstances. I thought to myself, *"If I go into Youth With A Mission, I will be happier."* But I wasn't sure if that was what God had for me. After three days of laying my requests out before the Lord, God spoke to my spirit, *"I want you in the church."* He said, *"I will give you all the discipleship training you need as you serve me."*

At age 21, I had no idea how the Lord would use me as a leader in the church or a missionary on short term trips. It pays to wait on the Lord for your answers. Sometimes we need to fast as well.[2] Fasting is hard for me even to this day because my body likes and needs food. But when I do fast, I am more in tune and sensitive to His voice. God was most likely trying to communicate with me all along, but my senses were dull to hear His voice. Fasting can help you get to a place to receive a clear and clean and pure word from God. This has been my personal experience. My recommendation is that we do fast, but not out of duty or obligation. Rather, we fast in response to a longing to connect with God's heart, to hear His voice, and to receive prophecy from a pure stream.

Remember our God is faithful. It says in the Bible that He will answer. Like Hannah, let us not be weary in pressing into His presence for our answers.

Declaration

Ask the Holy Spirit about writing out declarations and decrees you receive during your prayer time. He may want you to write down what He has already established as truth in the Bible, but He also wants released as a declaration. You may begin your announcement with full joy. A declaration is an announcement or a statement of something that you have decided upon as truth. For me, this is a powerful place in a prayer meeting or gathering of believers.

> *Habakkuk 2:2 "Then the LORD replied: 'Write down the revelation and make it plain on tablets so that a herald may run with it.'"*

When you are releasing a declaration, you are empowering what you know to be something God has established. Many times, the Holy Spirit will move on me during a worship service to read out a portion of scripture as a declaration of truth. The faith level in the room begins to rise. The company of worshipers becomes unified in God's intent for the service. When this happens, God begins to move in the house.

A piece of history most Americans are aware of is the war that was won in 1776. The Colonists were at war with England for their freedom to live in this new land, free from British rule. At one point, the scene painted before us shows Paul Revere riding through the town to warn the people of danger and tell them to get ready for a fight. He made a declaration, *"The British are coming! The British are coming!"* It was a declaration of war. The announcement stirred the necessary preparation needed for the Colonists to fight for their freedom.

A declaration is a noun and an adjective. You take a truth and speak it out loud, stating this information is so. Remember, this is happening in courts all the time. There are declarations and decrees even in the making of a law. The spiritual world understands laws and protocols. The demonic realm must abide by these laws. Think about the angel of death that was killing the firstborn sons in Egypt. If the blood of a spotless lamb was painted over the doorpost, that household was safe. The death angel could not enter.

Imagine having been in the room when the Declaration of Independence was written and signed. This document has been legal and binding for the United States of America; a country free from the rule of any other nation. The Declaration of Independence has been a compass that has guided us; a solid foundation on which our country has been built. This document has been used to establish the laws of the land and is used in our court systems every day. Thank God for the foresight these men had in the formation of this legal and binding document.

If forming a decree and declaration for our country's freedom has been so vital to establish our foundation as a nation, imagine if we as believers do the same in the spiritual realm through our prayers and worship. This should be taken into consideration in the songs we write and the words we speak over ourselves, our families, our cities, states and the nations of the world.

Decrees

The power in using decrees as a part of your prayer life is often overlooked. Whenever you see the word decree used in the Bible it is used as some type of legal term.

In the book of Daniel, King Darius issued a decree for the entire kingdom. If anyone prayed to another God but the king himself, they would be thrown into the lion's den.[3] If you've read the story, you already know Daniel ended up in the lion's den. A decree was made, and it stood as law once it was signed. A decree is an order or edict; it can also be a command or a mandate. A decree is used in a court of law to make a judgment or verdict.

In the book of Esther, we read how important a decree really is.[4] The story of Esther tells us about the courage of a young woman and her uncle Mordecai. Esther obeyed her uncle when he asked her to join with other young women in preparation to be chosen as queen. All the way through the process, Esther remains humble and obedient to both her uncle and those in charge of the preparation. This story is where the famous quote originated, *"And who knows but that you have come to your royal position for such a time as this?"* (Esther 4:14)

Esther was chosen out of all the beautiful maidens. It wasn't long before trouble began to brew in the Prussian Kingdom. Haman, who was second in command to the King, had an ego a mile long. Haman was angry that Mordecai would not bow before him. One day Haman had had enough. In his fury, he wrote a decree to annihilate all the Jews, responding in revenge to Mordecai's obstinate behavior. When Mordecai discovered this, he got word to Esther.

Esther sent the message out to her fellow Jews to join her in prayer and fasting in hopes to save herself and her people. After a three day fast of no water or food, God gave Esther wisdom and a strategy to appeal to the King. She served a banquet in which she invited Hamon to attend. Haman had no idea he was about to be exposed and the very gallows he had built for Mordecai would be used for his own execution.

Just before Esther exposed Haman, the King told her to ask for whatever she wanted, even up to half of the kingdom. Esther began to unravel Haman's plot. Esther asked the King to spare her people. The King granted her request and Haman and his household were hanged on the very gallows he built for Mordecai. Esther was allowed to rewrite a decree for her people that brought them safety and freedom.

We have a King. His name is Jesus. With His permission, we can also cancel the decree sent by the enemy, just as Esther did. This can extend beyond our own families as we intercede for nations and people groups around the world.

How do you know the enemy has an edict against you like Haman had written against Mordecai and the Jews? There are many ways to tell. First of all, you will sense the Holy Spirit nudging you in this direction. Or, maybe you might see your children struggling in unusual ways that don't seem to settle even after much prayer. The warfare will feel intense in many ways.

You may notice a negative pattern or cycle that keeps repeating itself. If this is the case, ask the Holy Spirit to help you write a decree for your family that releases life, purity, health and so on. Write this out with your spouse if you are married. Keep this decree in a place you will see it frequently. Read it out loud as a part of your prayer time.

The Kingdom of God operates in legal ways. The enemy is fully aware of God's protocols and knows he must also obey the rules. In Zechariah 3:1-10 we read about a courtroom scene in heaven. Satan accuses Joshua, the high priest, and the Lord God answers Satan's accusation.

His angels obey and assist the Lord. Joshua is released and cleansed for his earthly assignment.

If God says a thing, it stands. It is a heavenly decree that affects both the spiritual world and the natural world. The enemy must obey it. James says, *"Submit yourself therefore unto God, resist the enemy and he will flee."* [5] This is legally binding. Decrees that are written and led by the Holy Spirit will also be legally binding in the spiritual realm.

After I grabbed hold of the power of decrees in prayer, they began to transform my prayer life. I began to see my faith rise and prayers answered as I stood on God's Word and His promises. From this place, I could prophesy from a pure stream.

Activation Prayer:

Heavenly Father, I thank You that You are so gloriously intelligent. You are so smart that the enemy simply cannot keep up with You. I come before You now and ask You to teach me how to pray. I am asking You to teach me how to declare Your word and how to write out prayers and decrees for my family and all those things that concern me. Show me how to be a Mordecai or Esther of my time. Show me how to pray prayers that capture Your heart and cause the angels to pay attention, listen and act. Use my mouth to be a world changer in the privacy of my prayer closet. In Jesus' name. Amen.

Chapter Three
INTIMACY

Listening

In Song of Solomon, the display of poetic affection of the Lover for his Beloved is almost provocative. Some ask, *"How did this get in the Bible?"* Well if you've done any research on the topic of this book, you will find that most theologians agree that this love story is an allegory or reflection of our God's love for us.

If you view the book 'Song of Solomon' as a reflection of Christ's love for His bride, the Church, you can begin to see that the longing of the Bridegroom for his bride is Christ's heart for you. As I read the poetry between the lovers in this book, one word comes to mind, 'intimacy'.

Intimacy is one of the keys the Lord showed me for prophesying from a pure stream or flow with Jesus. How does one know if they are intimate with God, or their spouse for that matter? Intimacy at its root will reveal that you know details about the person you are in a relationship with that only come from time spent with them. This has been important to our God since the Garden of Eden. It is said in Genesis that God walked with Adam in the Garden of Eden in the cool of the day.

> Genesis 3:8 *"Then the man and his wife heard the sound of the LORD God as he was walking in the garden in the cool of the day, and they hid from the LORD God among the trees of the garden."*

The enemy has long been trying to interrupt our intimate connection with God. The enemy knows, if we are intimate with God, then we will truly know our God as well as ourselves as we are found in Him. You see, in knowing God and spending time with Him, you will also begin to know who you really are. This terrifies the enemy. If he can block or stop you from listening to and obeying the voice of God, he will. This was the known threat to the enemy in the Garden and is still to this day.

You receive prophetic words when you know God and listen to Him. Prophecy is knowing the heart of God on a matter. It often can be a word or picture of something that has happened, like a word of knowledge or something that is coming, a forthtelling or prophecy. It is about seeing others as He sees them. It's about helping us understand what He is doing and sometimes why He is doing it. Prophecy brings encouragement. It says to your soul, you matter, God sees you. God cares about what matters to His children. Hearing from God will increase your faith that God is alive and with you forever.

There is a book that influenced me greatly as a young adult. The book is called *Hearing Heart* by Hannah Hurnard.[1] Hannah Hurnard is the author of another well-known book titled *Hinds Feet on High Places*.[2] I read *Hinds Feet on High Places* and loved the tale she told of Little Miss Much Afraid and all the other characters whose names were descriptive of their character issues like Craven Fear and many others. So, when I saw *Hearing Heart* was an autobiography, I was intrigued.

I chose to take it with me during my first mission trip to Mexico City, Mexico. I will not be quoting from it, but I would like to share a nugget of truth I learned while reading the book. Here it is: To have a hearing heart, one must be listening. True listening is seen in the one who is obeying the Lord.

As a preschool teacher for many years, I learned the value of teaching the children to stop what they were doing and get quiet when I needed their attention. I would say *"listening ears."* This also meant the students were not to speak while I was talking. If they were busy talking to one another, they would completely miss what I was sharing with them. I discovered how well they could hear when they listened. How well they listened determined if they had the instructions required for the next activity. This skill taught in pre-school will carry them well through life.

God may be saying the same thing to us: *"Listening ears."* In other words, *"I have something to say and you could miss it if you are not listening."* If you are too busy talking or looking around at what others are doing, you could miss His voice.

What is He saying to you? How does He feel about your activities? Do you want to know? Do you want to know Him on an intimate level? God may be speaking to your heart and you do not know it because you are too busy with other things.

Remember the Bible story of the two sisters, Mary and Martha? Mary sat at Jesus' feet listening to His words while Martha ran around trying to prepare lunch.

> *Luke 10:38-42 "As Jesus and his disciples were on their way, he came to a village where a woman named Martha opened her home to him. She had a sister called Mary, who sat at the Lord's feet listening to what he said. But Martha was distracted by all the preparations that had to be made. She came to him and asked, 'Lord, don't you care that my sister has left me to do the work by myself? Tell her to help me!'*
>
> *'Martha, Martha,' the Lord answered, 'you are worried and upset about many things, but few things are needed—or indeed only one. Mary has chosen what is better, and it will not be taken away from her.'"*

There is nothing wrong with Martha's desire to feed everyone lunch. She had the problem herself. Her heart was getting resentful for her labor while she was missing out on a moment she would never get back; a moment to sit at Jesus' feet. When we listen, we better recognize the moment when all that is needed is to sit quietly at the feet of our Master. Soak in His presence as you learn from Him.

There are a couple of great songs that come to mind on this topic. They both describe the beauty in having a desire to be close and intimate with our Lord. The first song is *In the Secret,* written by Andy Park.[3] The second is *The More I Seek You,* written by Zac Neese.[4] I encourage you to listen to these songs and others like them to inspire your longing for time with Him.

What's in There?

It is so important that we check our hearts with the Lord to see if there is anything that could be blocking our relationship. David understood this. He wrote about it in the book of Psalms, *"Create in me a clean heart and renew a right spirit in me."*[5] Closeness or intimacy with God is so much better with a clean heart. All negative or dark attitudes have been confessed, forgiven and removed through the blood of Jesus and our confession.

> *Psalm 51:10-12 "Create in me a pure heart, O God, and renew a steadfast spirit within me. Do not cast me from your presence or take your Holy Spirit from me. Restore to me the joy of your salvation and grant me a willing spirit, to sustain me."*

Intimacy with God thrives when there are no offenses or frustrations hindering our attention when we meet with Him in prayer or worship. The open and tender heart is much freer to give and receive. The Sermon on the Mount is a perfect place in scripture to hear the heart of the Father through His Son, Jesus, as He taught us a different way to think. In every one of the beatitudes, Jesus was dealing with the question, *"Where is your heart?"* In Matthew, chapters 5, 6 and 7, He is speaking of heart issues.

> *Matthew 5:3-12 "Blessed are the poor in spirit, for theirs is the kingdom of Heaven. Blessed are those who mourn, for they will be comforted. Blessed are the meek, for they will inherit the earth. Blessed are those who hunger and thirst for righteousness, for they will be filled.*
>
> *Blessed are the merciful, for they will be shown mercy. Blessed are the pure in heart, for they will see God. Blessed are the*

peacemakers, for they will be called children of God. Blessed are those who are persecuted because of righteousness, for theirs is the kingdom of Heaven.

Blessed are you when people insult you, persecute you and falsely say all kinds of evil against you because of me. Rejoice and be glad, because great is your reward in Heaven, for in the same way they persecuted the prophets who were before you."

I would like to add my own beatitude: *Blessed are you when you allow the Holy Spirit to search your heart. For in so doing, your intimacy with the Lord and others will increase.*

When my children were growing up, they would attend a yearly Christian camp called 'Go Camp.' This was a week-long camp held at a church. Some years, the camp was for the whole family with children of all ages and other years the focus would only be on the youth in attendance. The point of the camp was to train the children/ youth in growing their relationship with Jesus. We would take them on outreaches so they could learn to be bold in sharing their faith. During these outreaches, the children would perform songs and dance along with skits that conveyed the message of the gospel.

Something they always did at Go Camp before going on any outreach to the community was a heart check. The leader made time for the kids to speak to any person they had been hurt by or were angry with. The point of doing this was to be certain there was nothing standing in the way of clear communication between themselves and God as well as each other. They wanted to be certain the enemy could not get the upper hand before going out to reach the people in the community.

The interesting truth is that having anger or frustrations with anyone will create this invisible wall between God and each other. There is a reason the apostle Paul said, "Do not let the sun go down on your anger." And in another verse Paul warned husbands not to be harsh with their wife so that their prayers would not be hindered.

> *Ephesians 4:26-27 "In your anger do not sin. Do not let the sun go down while you are still angry, and do not give the devil a foothold."*

> *1 Peter 3:7 "Husbands, in the same way be considerate as you live with your wives, and treat them with respect as the weaker partner and as heirs with you of the gracious gift of life, so that nothing will hinder your prayers."*

It is a delight to go before the Lord and allow Him to create a clean heart within us. It is a wonderful feeling when you know your consciousness is clear before your God and your fellow man. It is like going to the dentist for a teeth cleaning. You know there will be no drilling or pain. And you get to leave the office with squeaky clean teeth.

Time

Time is one of the most precious resources we have. How we choose to spend our time will impact the quality of our lives. It will affect everything. Are we moving forward towards our dreams or are we stuck in the rut of excess wasted time? I was listening to the radio and heard the announcer speak kindly about a recent death of a celebrity. When this celebrity knew he was dying and had his loved ones surrounding his deathbed, he quietly uttered, *"So much wasted time."*

Equally important to how we spend our time is whom we choose to spend our time with. There is a saying that you become like those you spend the most time with. Have you ever noticed older couples that have been married for many years seem to finish each other's sentences? They seem to know what each other is thinking before a word is even spoken. The couples that have spent time together seem to be in rhythm and have an inner quiet about them regardless of what situation surrounds them. Not so with newly married couples, in general, who have not had the benefit of undistracted time together.

I used to get a kick out of watching the old game show *The Newlywed Game*. The host would send either the husbands or wives backstage and begin to ask personal questions of the spouse left onstage. It was so funny to see the reactions of the spouses when they returned. Their partners' answers were often hilarious and not accurate at all. Of course, this is what made the show so much fun to watch.

You become who you spend time with. My grandmother used to tell me all the time, *"Birds of a feather flock together."* She also said, *"It only takes one bad apple to spoil the whole bunch."* At the time, I did not yet see the value in her words. Grandma was giving me very important truths to set me on a good course for the rest of my life.

> *1 Corinthians 15:33 "Do not be misled: bad company corrupts good character."*

If bad company corrupts good character, then it stands to reason that good company builds good character. One of the ways we build good character is by reading books by authors that motivate us in our walk with the Lord. There are so many wonderful books on just about any topic that can equip us on our journey. Nothing, of course, replaces the scriptures. The Bible is our plumb line. It's our blueprint for knowing God and making Him known.

I have many mentors that I do not know personally, but I know them through their books and the teachings they have available on the web, through podcasts or C.D.'s. These mentors are for the purpose of my growth. We are so blessed to live during such a time as this when there is a banquet table of teaching and training materials just a click away. What about quality time? We can spend time with the Lord, but also be so distracted with our mental to do lists that we are not really focused on Him. We do this with people also.

Years ago, I started doing something to help with distractions during my prayer time. In the back of my journal, I set up a to do section to write out whatever task popped into my head. This way, when my mind wandered, I wouldn't stay distracted or worry about forgetting something. When I write the thought down in the back of my prayer journal, I can get back to praying. This really helps me. Just simply having a piece of paper to jot thoughts down will do the same thing. I personally like to journal my prayer time with the Lord. It is so fun to read later and see all the prayers that have been answered.

I enjoy having a friend invite me out for lunch, especially if we haven't spent time together in a while. After we get settled at our table and have placed our orders, with the general greetings aside, we begin to share our hearts. We get caught up on what is happening in each other's lives with laughter, smiles, and a genuine connection.

I have also seen the following scenario while dining out. The person I was with was preoccupied with their cell phone. Instead of talking to me and sharing in each other's lives, we both end up staring at our electronics. The point is, it is not enough that you are just spending time with each other. The time together should be quality time by both being present and engaged with the other person. The goal is to have a real connection.

I remember when I first rededicated my life to the Lord. I was so hungry for the Word. I would bring my Bible with me wherever I went. On my lunch breaks at work, I could not wait to run out to my car and read the Bible and talk to God. I would even hold my Bible to my lips and kiss it to thank God for speaking to men and inspiring those who wrote what God had spoken to them.

Time spent in the Word propelled me into a deeper spiritual understanding of who Jesus was for me and created a deeper intimacy in my life with my God. This was and still is a delight to my heart.

Atmosphere

Atmosphere is important. We are all affected by it for good or not so good. If I do not get the dinner dishes done before going to bed at night, I will wake up in the morning to a pile of last night's mess. This has not proven to be the best way for me to start my day. I might be tempted to grumble at the pile up in my sink and on the counters. Worse yet, my husband will grumble, and I do not want that. But if I take the time the night before and get the kitchen nice and clean, it looks so inviting in the morning. What a great atmosphere for my morning cup of tea as I pull out my Bible and spend time with Jesus.

When you read the Old Testament, you will notice there were clear-cut instructions for the builders of the ark of the covenant. God had the builders use a certain type of wood and the measurements had to be perfect. Remember, God used to dwell in the ark. He required an atmosphere that was conducive to carrying His presence.

Things have changed since the life, death and resurrection of Jesus Christ. The Bible teaches us that we are now the temple of God. God chose to dwell in us. This is incredible. The children of God used to carry the ark so His presence was with them wherever they would go. It is a wonderful truth, that God is not in one location anymore, but He is everywhere inhabiting all his born-again believers.

1 Corinthians 3:16 "Don't you know that you yourselves are God's temple and that God's Spirit dwells in your midst?"

Colossians 1:27 "To them God has chosen to make known among the Gentiles the glorious riches of this mystery, which is Christ in you, the hope of glory."

The beautiful truth is that the Spirit of God now lives in you. Because of this, you are His atmosphere carrier. That is why we must be careful what we watch on television or what music we listen to. We are now His temple and we want to maintain a clear frequency channel with our God. We want to hear Him clearly and know Him well and, then, make Him known to others.

Atmosphere can enhance your intimate time with the Lord. Sometimes, we just need to get away from all the noise and the everyday demands. I dream of having my own property one day where I can create a place to meet with the Lord. I treasure the beauty of nature. Because of this, my favorite way to spend time with God is in nature. I would like to share this special place with others so that they too can enjoy the beauty of nature and the presence of God.

Imagine yourself with your Bible, a notebook and pen, looking out over a beautiful water scene or mountain view. There is a bench or hammock waiting there for you. You breathe in, you breathe out and you wait in the peaceful presence of the Lord, prepared and ready to listen for His voice.

I had a friend who would create the most beautiful settings for her friends using fabrics, pillows and other décor. She would make a tent for those who desired to go inside and spend private time with Jesus. When you walked into the tent, you never wanted to leave. It was wonderful to be in that setting and enjoy that intimacy with the Lord. She understood the importance of creating a quiet place to meet with God. My friend taught me that atmosphere is something that can be created thus minimizing distractions. This leaves your soul at peace and rest to receive from the Lord.

Aglow International understands this well. For every conference they hold, there is a team of men and women who set up a "quiet place" or prayer room. It is not there for you to get prayer from another person, that happens in a completely different room. This is a place for you to meet with God alone. Bethel Church in Redding California has such a place created by Beni Johnson and her team. It is a 24-hour prayer room, set apart from the main building. Worship music plays 24/7. There is a water feature in the center of the room. Also, many pillows are provided for those who enjoy laying in His presence.

In atmospheres such as the ones described, I always receive downloads from the Holy Spirit. It is important to bring a journal along with a pen, because you don't want to forget a word the Lord speaks.

Activation Prayer:

Heavenly Father, I love Your presence. To spend time with You is my heart's delight. Help me to learn how to establish an atmosphere that cultivates my time with You. Thank You, Jesus, for giving me "listening ears". Thank You for helping me to stop and listen to what You are saying.

Jesus, I choose to set aside time for us to be together. I want to know Your heart. I want to know what makes You smile as well as what grieves Your heart. Search my heart, Lord. Remove anything that would stand in the way of our communication. You are my God and I adore You. Teach me to prophesy from a pure stream, in Jesus' name. Amen.

Chapter Four

FORGIVENESS

Offenses

Living this life, we are given the opportunity to take up offenses. The world is riddled with this nasty disease. In fact, unforgiveness is considered one of the contributing factors to both sickness and disease. This is a medically documented fact. If you don't believe me, look it up on the internet or take a trip to the library. Unforgiveness hurts our body, soul and spirit. When we harbor offenses in our heart, it also contaminates the body and soul. The topic of forgiveness was an important part of Jesus' messages while He walked this earth. His words still ring true today.

Mathew 6:14-15 "For if you forgive other people when they sin against you, your Heavenly Father will also forgive you. But if you do not forgive others their sins, your Father will not forgive your sins."

Even though God's mercy is profound and limitless, Jesus said that your sins would not be forgiven if you do not forgive others. This is not an easy word to hear, especially if you have been robbed of your dignity, your innocence, your property, or your reputation. It is very hard to let go of unforgiveness. Sometimes unforgiveness can feel like false justification. We can talk ourselves into all the reasons why we should not forgive the offender. Remember, true justice comes from the Lord.

Matthew 18:21-22 "Then Peter came to Jesus and asked, 'Lord, how many times shall I forgive my brother or sister who sins against me? Up to seven times?' Jesus answered, 'I tell you, not seven times, but seventy-seven times.'"

I do not think that was the answer Peter was expecting. I imagine Peter got very quiet after Jesus spoke those words to him. Perhaps he began to think, *"How on earth am I supposed to do that?"*

After Jesus spoke to him about this, he then began to teach:

Matthew 18:23-35 "Therefore, the kingdom of Heaven is like a king who wanted to settle accounts with his servants. As he began the settlement, a man who owed him ten thousand bags of gold was brought to him. Since he was not able to pay, the master ordered that he and his wife and his children and all that he had be sold to repay the debt.

At this the servant fell on his knees before him. 'Be patient with me,' he begged, 'and I will pay back everything.' The servant's master took pity on him, canceled the debt and let him go.

But when that servant went out, he found one of his fellow servants who owed him a hundred silver coins. He grabbed him and began to choke him. 'Pay back what you owe me!' he demanded.

His fellow servant fell to his knees and begged him, 'Be patient with me, and I will pay it back.'

But he refused. Instead, he went off and had the man thrown into prison until he could pay the debt. When the other servants saw what had happened, they were outraged and went and told their master everything that had happened.

Then the master called the servant in. 'You wicked servant,' he said, 'I canceled all that debt of yours because you begged me to. Shouldn't you have had mercy on your fellow servant just as I had on you?' In anger his master handed him over to the jailers to be tortured, until he should pay back all he owed.

This is how my Heavenly Father will treat each of you unless you forgive your brother or sister from your heart."

We all need forgiveness. Often, we offend someone without even realizing it. Maybe we are the one who accidentally cut someone off while driving. I know I have. I've heard a horn honk behind me, or someone flipped me off and I have no idea why. This stuff can happen on the home front also. Since we want to have others show us gracious kindness when we make a mistake, shouldn't we offer this to others as well? God is generous with mercy and forgiveness which He gives to us. He requires that we do the same to others.

There was a time when I was so broken. I was in so much emotional pain from hurt that transpired in my marriage, I wanted to be angry and I felt I had a right to be. One day I was in the kitchen chopping vegetables on the cutting board. With each slice of the knife I mumbled to myself some of the things my husband had done that really hurt me.

I heard the voice of the Lord speak, *"Sin is crouching at your door, it desires to have you, you must master it."*

I was suddenly very quiet. I knew that God, by his Spirit, spoke to me. He was gently telling me that I must forgive my husband. *"It's not fair, God,"* I said out loud. *"This really hurts."*

Later that night, while at our marriage class, one of the leaders said, *"I keep hearing the Lord tell me to read a portion of Scripture."*

He began to read:

> *Genesis 4:6-7 "Then the Lord said to Cain, 'Why are you angry? Why is your face downcast? If you do what is right, will you not be accepted? But if you do not do what is right, sin is crouching at your door; it desires to have you, but you must rule over it.'"*

Our leader explained that he felt this passage of scripture had to do with forgiveness. He explained that Cain had offenses against his brother. I raise my hand and shared with the group what God had told me earlier. The group prayed for me and for our marriage. They thanked me for my honesty and acknowledged the battle is real. In that moment, my eyes were opened to the demonic activity behind unforgiveness. Sin was active, moving, and crouching at my door. I had real things to forgive. Troubles in our marriage were real, but I began to see how the enemy was actively keeping me bound in my thought life with pain and unforgiveness.

Steve and I needed to cooperate with the instructions of the Lord. When God spoke *"You need to forgive"*, it was important that I acted on that in order to move forward in the healing and restoration of our marriage. It was so hard to completely forgive in that moment; but once I let it go, I also realized that I was accountable just for myself and not for my husband. He was accountable for himself to the Lord. This set me free, and my intimacy with the Lord was restored. Thank You, Jesus. God also fully restored our marriage. Our God is faithful.

Holding a Grudge

Forgiving quickly when you are hurt or offended will prevent you from the temptation to hold a grudge. When my children were young, we needed to talk about this from time to time. These conversations happened, especially if one of the children hurt, bothered or offended the other sibling.

Definition of grudge from the online urban dictionary[1]:

1. A grudge is a bad feeling or hate you hold against another person for something bad they did, or you think they did, to you.
2. A feeling of anger or resentment that you hold against a specific person for something they did that angered you in the past.

It's interesting to look at the urban dictionary online and read the varying definitions of the word "grudge." I could easily see someone walking into a classroom of students and asking them for their definition. A sort of children's urban dictionary would be enlightening, I think. I have a feeling the details may vary from grade to grade, but the main point would stay the same. A grudge is unforgiveness towards someone who hurts your heart.

There were times I was worn out by the things my children chose to bicker about. I wanted them to learn how to problem solve themselves, but they seemed to like the security of having Mom come in as the just judge. There were often injustices happening as each child learned the art of preferring one another. Sometimes, they would be so very angry. As a mom, my job seemed to be to first listen to their woes, then to redirect their focus off the anger into the action stage of what they could do to help repair the relationship. Holding on to offenses can turn into a grudge. If not forgiven, a grudge becomes a bitter root. Bitter roots are very hard to get rid of.

I was leading worship at one of the local Aglow meetings. Out of the blue, I heard the Lord speak to me. He said, *"You have unforgiveness in your heart"*. I was shocked at this because I always try to keep short accounts with anyone who hurts me. I asked the Lord, *"How do I have unforgiveness in my heart and who do I have it with?"* The Lord answered, *"You have unforgiveness in your heart towards the terrorist group that has been so destructive."* I knew instantly that it was true.

I had been recently watching the news and ranting on about how awful these people were. I had taken up an offense against them and I was allowing it to turn into a grudge. When I prayed for them to be caught, it was with a strong sense of eagerness for God to give them what they deserved. This area has a fine balance for us to walk. Jesus told us to love our enemies and pray for those who persecute us. If you are in a place of holding their sin against them, you will be like James and John who asked permission to call down fire on those they deemed deserving of punishment.

> *Luke 9:54-56 (KJV) "And when his disciples James and John saw this, they said, Lord, wilt thou that we command fire to come down from Heaven, and consume them, even as Elias did? But he turned, and rebuked them, and said, Ye know*

not what manner of spirit ye are of. For the Son of man is not come to destroy men's lives, but to save them. And they went to another village."

We have read many times that King David felt this way about his enemies.[2] The Father understands but He sent His Son Jesus to show us there is a better way. As the worship continued, I felt led to share with the group what the Lord was revealing to me. As I did, you know what? Many in the room nodded their heads in agreement. They had struggled with the same thing and saw their need to forgive as well. Together, as a company of men and women, we first asked the Lord for the forgiveness of hardened hearts against this group. Doing this released us from a potential bitter root.

We then began to pray for the terrorists. We prayed they would have visions and dreams of Jesus in the night. We asked God to encounter them with His love, knowing love must replace hate in order to stop the hurtful destruction against humanity. We prayed that every plan of the enemy to destroy an innocent one would be exposed, brought to light and stopped by those in authority.

Now, that is a much more productive way to live. Instead of holding offenses, we release and forgive them. Then our hearts remain clean, and God has a chance to use our prayers for change where change needs to happen. I will close this section with the words of Jesus.

Matthew 5:43-47 "You have heard that it was said, 'Love your neighbor and hate your enemy.' But I tell you, love your enemies and pray for those who persecute you, that you may be children of your Father in Heaven. He causes his sun to rise on the evil and the good, and sends rain on the righteous and the unrighteous. If you love those who love you, what reward will you get? Are not even the tax collectors doing that? And if you greet only your own people, what are you doing more than others? Do not even pagans do that?"

Bitterness

Bitterness is the last stage of evidence that you have unforgiveness. When you reach this stage, a root has taken place in your soul that is often difficult to remove. When this happens, it is very hard to hear God clearly. It is almost impossible to prophesy from a pure stream. Think about weeds in your yard. One of the most commonly known is the dandelion. Now I know there are benefits to these plants, like making dandelion tea. But for the sake of an analogy, we are going to look at them as most do. They are weeds.

Folks are forever trying to get dandelions out of their yards. When you mow them down, you don't see the flowering weed for a while, but before you know it, there it is again. That bright yellow flower is a reminder that this weed is hard to get rid of. To make matters worse, this weed is full of seeds with a taproot system that keeps them multiplying around your yard. Even when you try to pull this weed out of the ground by its roots, you will not succeed. It will always break off because the roots of these lovely weeds grow deep and anchor tightly to the soil beneath.

This is what the enemy tries to do in the soil of your heart. One of the enemies' primary tactics is to feed you lies. He will whisper in your ear and remind you of all the reasons why you should not forgive. Remember my story in the offense portion of this chapter? This is precisely what the enemy was doing to me as I was chopping my vegetables. He was reminding me of all the reasons I needed to stay angry.

Ephesians 4:31-32 "Get rid of all bitterness, rage and anger, brawling and slander, along with every form of malice.' 'Be kind and compassionate to one another, forgiving each other, just as in Christ, God forgave you."

According to scriptures, a bitter root can affect many.

Hebrews 12:15 "See to it that no one falls short of the grace of God and that no bitter root grows up to cause trouble and defile many."

I understand that this verse has greater implications like falling short of God's grace by false teachings and the worship of idols. When we allow a bitter root to form in our hearts, could we be trying to become our own god rather than trusting the Lord to heal us and take care of the painful situation?

Deuteronomy 29:18 "Make sure there is no man or woman, clan or tribe among you today whose heart turns away from the LORD our God to go and worship the gods of those nations; make sure there is no root among you that produces such bitter poison."

I need to ask, *"When you or someone you know has a bitter root, do you think it will bear the fruit of the Spirit or the fruit of the flesh?"*

I propose that we get rid of sin that can hinder us from running the race with boldness, confidence and a pure connection with God.

We can find bitter roots in wars of many kinds. One example is found in race wars. The bitterness spreads from the parents to the children. Left unchecked, the end result is hatred and violence. I have been a victim of race wars. During the late 60's, things were getting really stirred up in our country. Martin Luther King, Jr. had been killed and more violence erupted in the streets.

There were good reasons to be angry and protest for change was needed. There were great injustices that needed repair. As a young child, I had to walk to school because my mom had three other children not yet school aged at home. As I was walking to school, a young black girl began to yell at me, *"You called me nigger!"* Over and over, she yelled this lie, and I began to cry.

I answered, *"Jesus loves all the children of the world. I would never say that to you."*

The girl then began to call me a liar and threw me against a rock wall as if I were a rag doll. No matter what I said, the girl would not believe me. Instead of walking to school, I walked home in tears. There would be many more negative experiences that happened to me before we moved away.

It is important that you forgive anyone that has hurt or harmed you or your fellow man, to keep your children and your children's children free from the root of bitterness. In so doing, you maintain a pure flow from your heart to God's. This pure stream will benefit generations to come.

There was a young man whose mother passed away. Just as his mother breathed her last breath, his much older brother came into the room where the mother was lying, and said, *"We need to talk about the will."* The mother had wanted her youngest son to receive her home as an inheritance. It was a small home, but she felt it would help her youngest son get started in life.

All her sons had witnessed her speaking of this as her heart's desire. She had spoken about it to all her children, but the cancer took her away before she was able to see her attorney and officially change her will. Even though the whole family including extended family knew of her desire to help her youngest son in this way, it did not change the fact that the will was legal and binding.

So, the older son, who wanted his fair share and who didn't cooperate with what everyone knew was his mother's desire, got his way in the end. The law is the law. Now this young man could have gone to court over the matter of a verbal will, but he knew it would produce only more pain and heartache. Not to mention the great cost, which was money he did not have.

The youngest son carried on with life and raised his family. Deep down, every time he thought about how his older brother had handled the will, it caused him great pain. He could not talk about his mother's passing without bringing up what his older brother had done. One night after several years had gone by, he had a dream. In the dream the Lord revealed how his heart had grown bitter. The Lord revealed that this bitterness had hurt his marriage and his relationship with God.

When the youngest son realized what he had allowed to happen in his heart, he humbly asked the Lord for forgiveness. He also forgave his older brother for everything. When an opportunity presented itself, the younger son was able to meet with his older brother free of any feelings of resentment or anger. He was free, and a lost relationship was found again.

Are You Still Talking About It?

I have had people ask me a question numerous times over the years, *"How do I know if I have really forgiven?"* They ask, *"Jesus said to forgive seventy times seven so does that mean I need to daily forgive a person for the same thing I already forgave them for?"*

I often answer with this statement. *"A sign that you have forgiven someone is that you no longer feel a need to discuss what they did to you or how you feel about them or the situation anymore."*

Luke 6:45 "A good man brings good things out of the good stored up in his heart, and an evil man brings evil things out of the evil stored up in his heart. For the mouth speaks what the heart is full of."

Have you ever noticed that when you have been emotionally wounded, you often feel the need to talk about it? This principle applies with forgiveness too; what is in your heart and thoughts will eventually be spoken out loud. Sharing your heart and your pain can be very healthy. What is not healthy, however, is when talking about the pain only builds up more frustration. The more you talk about it, the angrier you become. Your mind relives the hurtful events every time you speak about it. Reliving your hurt by talking about it over and over can be detrimental to your body. This is scientifically proven. I will address this in greater detail later in this book.

When my husband and I were struggling in our marriage, I often wanted to talk about my pain and struggles that I was going through with one or more of my closest friends. It would have been fine if I had asked for prayer and left my pain on the altar with Jesus. But this is not what would happen. I would go on and on about what my husband had said or done and how it had wounded me. By the time I was ready to hang up the phone, I felt worse than I had before I called. I asked myself, *"Why would this be? Isn't it healthy to get everything off your chest?"*

I discovered that instead of feeling better after talking to my friend, I felt worse. I realized that I needed to stop talking about it. My job was to forgive and release my husband. I needed to work on communication with him and not complain about him to my best friend. I now believe that every time I would complain to my friend, I was not only reliving the memory and feeling the pain all over again, but I was attracting the demonic realm right into my home. Oh yes, the demonic is attracted to complaining like rats to garbage. I learned to allow the Lord to heal my heart and if I needed prayer or counsel, it was just that.

Now, I want to add, that if you have forgiven and yet it feels like your thoughts are still not free or that what they did or said keeps replaying in your mind, sometimes you need to break a soul tie with a person that has hurt you. This can even happen with the people closest to you. The topic of unhealthy soul ties can be hard to explain, but the truth is, we can become connected with the offender due to the wounding in an unhealthy way, depending on how extreme the wounding is or was. Now the Bible speaks of David and Jonathan having their souls knit together, which is another way of saying they had a soul tie.[3]

> *1 Samuel 18:1 (KJV) "And it came to pass, when he had made an end of speaking unto Saul, that the soul of Jonathan was knit with the soul of David, and Jonathan loved him as his own soul."*

The Bible alludes to this as a healthy tie, not an unhealthy one. But we can develop unhealthy, co-dependent soul ties. Once these are broken, both parties are released and freed. I have heard testimony after testimony of people breaking an unhealthy soul tie. Not only do they feel freer, but, to their surprise, when they see the person again, that person has changed for the better.

I knew one woman who grew up always feeling slightly rejected by her father. As a little girl, it looked as if the father preferred the older sister. The father was always pouring out praises upon her sister. As this little girl grew into a woman, she subconsciously looked for daddy's approval through other men. Also, when she would enter a married relationship with a man, he would ultimately reject her through acts of adultery. She ended up being married several times and never felt 'loved'.

While this woman was receiving personal prayer for inner healing, it was revealed that she might have unhealthy soul ties with her earthly father. She prayed with the minister and renounced any unhealthy soul ties, then asked Jesus to cut the soul tie. She forgave and released her father for unmet needs. She then asked the Lord to return any part of her that her father had retained and that it would be sent back to her through the blood of Jesus. She prayed that any part of him that she had retained be sent back to him through the cleansing blood of Jesus. The goal is for both people to be fully restored and made whole.

After this woman prayed this with the minister, she felt lighter. She noticed a heaviness was lifted off her shoulders. She was so excited about how she felt that she went to visit her father. She wanted to see if she noticed anything had changed between them, and it had. He spoke to her so tenderly and showed genuine appreciation toward her. This woman walked away full of the awe and wonder of God's goodness to her.

Breaking a soul tie does not always show itself this quickly in the other person, but it will in you. Sometimes the person stays mean or negative towards you. This does not happen often, but just in case it does, you will not be caught off guard. Understand, it is the enemy at work. The amazing thing is that you are free, and their negative behavior no longer brings you down as it once did.

Activation Prayer:

Heavenly Father, thank You for sending Your Son, Jesus, who paid the price for the forgiveness of my sin through His shed blood. Thank You, Jesus, for making a way for me and all mankind by allowing Yourself to be nailed to that cross. There is such power in Your blood, Jesus. I ask now that You would show me any area in my heart where I have unforgiveness towards anyone (wait for a moment for the Lord to show you who you may need to forgive or who you may need to ask forgiveness from).

Jesus, I ask You to remove any bitter roots from my heart and cleanse me from them now in Your name. I repent for taking my complaints to my friends instead of You, Lord. I ask You to heal my heart as I choose to forgive those who sinned against me, and that You would break off any ungodly soul ties I may have had with that person. I ask that You send back to them any part of them that I retained. Send it back through the cleansing blood of Jesus Christ. I also ask that You send back to me any part of me that they retained. Send it back through the cleansing blood of Jesus Christ. I thank You for breaking this soul tie off of me today. In the name of Jesus. Amen.

Chapter Five
LOVE

Fruit

There is nothing like a tasty piece of fruit, especially on a warm day. A fresh peach or a crisp apple is so refreshing and fulfilling to all five senses. Artists for centuries have painted beautiful baskets of ripe fruit for the viewer to enjoy and display on the walls of their homes. When you see a fruit basket full of color and variety, anticipation for the taste and texture forms in your mind.

Have you ever reached for an apple expecting to encounter the crisp juicy, crunchy taste and texture only to bite into mush? I think most of us have experienced that disappointment a time or two.

The same can be true with people. They look pleasant enough but if you accidently disappoint them, you will quickly see the fruit of their character. If the first reaction from them is to snap at you or talk down to you, it's clear this person needs more of the Holy Spirit to help them cultivate good fruit in their life. How wonderful it is when you are handled with kindness, patience and quickly forgiven. It is comparable to tasting delicious fruit. I think that may be one reason why the Lord had Paul use the term "fruit" as a comparative to the fruit of the Spirit.

> *Galatians 5:22-23 "But the fruit of the Spirit is love, joy, peace, forbearance, kindness, goodness, faithfulness, gentleness and self-control. Against such things there is no law."*

It's important to know what your strengths and weaknesses are and what fruits of the Spirit you need more of in your life. To say you are weak in an area simply means you acknowledge you are a human being who needs strength and growth. You are created in God's image. Thus, the Creator has given you an ability to tap into His greater strength.

> *2 Corinthians 12:9-10 "But he said to me, 'My grace is sufficient for you, for my power is made perfect in weakness.' Therefore, I will boast all the more gladly about my weaknesses, so that Christ's power may rest on me.... when I am weak then I am strong."*

I had a gentleman share a part of his story with me. As a young father coming home from work tired and worn every night, he would be greeted by his children with happy running feet reaching the door as fast as they could and full of excitement to see him. He would try to muster the same joy through his fatigue as they had been expressing. Following hugs all around, together they would run a bath for daddy's nightly soak.

As time went on, the young father noticed the children stopped coming to the door to greet him. In fact, it seemed he was ignored upon entrance. The father was perplexed. Why had his children lost interest in his return each night? He asked his wife what she thought might be going on with the kids.

His wife shared with him that every time he came home, he pointed out everything that was wrong in the house. He noticed and pointed out anything out of place. If there were any toys on the floor instead of making a game out of picking them up, he began to yell at his children to pick up their toys. His wife shared that the children were aware that they needed to pick up before he came home, but sometimes forgot because they were caught up in their play.

She suggested, *"Maybe you should focus on seeing your children and overlooking any messes until after dinner."*

The father began to inspect his fruit. He realized he had gotten lax with spending time with the Lord in the morning. He also realized he no longer felt patient, or even kind when he came home, but rather he felt edgy. He was just plain tired and lacked self-control. He felt remorse and told his kids he was going to work on coming home with a better attitude. He discovered that spending time, even fifteen minutes in the morning reading his Bible and talking to God, made all the difference. Plus, the awareness itself helped too.

His children agreed they would work on picking up their toys when they were finished playing with them rather than leaving them on the floor. There were hugs all around, and the family was restored to its happy place again.

> *Luke 6:43-44 "No good tree bears bad fruit, nor does a bad tree bear good fruit. Its own fruit recognizes each tree. People do not pick figs from thorn bushes, or grapes from briers."*

I believe Jesus taught His followers to look for fruit that comes from God, not just words or works like the Pharisee. Think about receiving a prophetic word from a person who you know has bad fruit in their life. You may doubt if the word they gave you is from God because you know this person has a problem with bitterness, anger, or pride. Compare that to the person giving you a word who has good fruit in their life and is known for their love and kindness. You are more apt to receive this word with confidence because the giver of the word reflects God's goodness. You can trust that the person with good fruit is more apt to give you a word from a pure stream.

> John 15:16 "You did not choose me, but I chose you and appointed you so that you might go and bear fruit—fruit that will last—and so that whatever you ask in my name the Father will give you."

As a young Christian woman, my desire was to please the Lord, and it still is. But I really struggled with my self-image. I had always been petite but after making positive changes in my life, which included quitting smoking cigarettes, I began to gain weight. I replaced cigarettes with sugar which resulted in weight gain. For the first time in my life, I had a weight problem. I began to cry out to God for help and He took me on a journey of discovering the fruit of the spirit and how each fruit represents an aspect of God's character. On this journey, I learned about self-control and I learned to love myself just the way I was, because God loved me.

Eventually, the weight came off, and I learned to keep it off by leaning into the Word of God for my life and body. I allowed the Holy Spirit to transform my mind through His powerful grace. The biggest weapon the enemy used against me at that time was condemnation.

Know this, the Lord leads us into repentance for our benefit, but He never condemns us. The enemy condemns us by feeding us his lies. When you become aware of how powerful grace is in your life, you will stop striving and allow the Lord to do the work. Before you know it, you are a tree planted by the waters bearing a bounty of fruit that brings glory to God.

Honor

What comes to mind when you hear the word "honor"? What do you see in your mind's eye when you read the word "honor"? Honor is a powerful word and it is very important to implement in your life. It was and is important enough to the Lord that it is used in the ten commandments, *"Honor your father and your mother, so that you may live long in the land the LORD your God is giving you"* (Exodus 20:12).

Honor is one of the keys to prophesy from a pure stream. As you walk in honor toward God and your fellow man, you will hear the Lord more clearly. Why? Because you are walking as Jesus walked. Honor is a demonstration of love. When you read about love in the Bible, you will get a clearer picture of what honor looks like.

Let's look at traditional marriage vows. They go something like this, *"Will you take this woman/man to be your wife/husband, to live together in holy marriage? Will you love her/him, comfort her/him, honor, and keep her/him in sickness and in health, and forsaking all others, be faithful to her/him as long as you both shall live?"*

There is honor in the display of love one for another. In honoring a person, you recognize that person has value. Honor is when you prefer someone above yourself. Let's say you are in a grocery store line buying a few things for lunch that day. You are in a hurry, but you notice the person behind you seems a little stressed. It's possible they are running late or are going through a tough time.

You never know what the person in front of you or behind you is going through. If you notice this, why not allow the other person to go in front of you? This act of kindness is twofold; it is honoring them as an individual, and by preferring them, you are honorable in your character.

The definition of honor is: "Honesty, fairness, or integrity in one's beliefs and actions to hold in honor or high respect; revere: to treat with honor."[1]

Whenever I am in a conversation with someone who shares their frustrations about another person, their church or boss; I like to ask a question. It's not for condemnation, but for motivation. The question is, *"What are you doing to help the situation?"* So often, you may think it is the other person who needs to change, but maybe God wants to use this to bring change in your life?

When dealing with people problems, the number one book I recommend for folks to read is *Culture of Honor* by Danny Silk.[2] This book is rich with examples of what honor looks like and what a kingdom minded church should look like. Danny Silk advocates that God is free to move in a culture of honor. A culture of honor looks like lives being transformed, and a place where bodies and minds are healed. He recognizes honor is a key.

Recognizing the gifts and unique qualities in an individual is one way to honor them. I remember my high school choir teacher. She was the one teacher who truly demonstrated honor for her students. *What? Her students? Shouldn't it be the other way around? Shouldn't the students honor the teacher?* Yes, the students should honor their teacher, but how will they learn to honor if it is never demonstrated? How will they know what honor looks like if no one models it?

This teacher valued and honored each student. She had an art for pulling out the gold in her choir members and was ready to encourage them whenever possible. She would often recognize leadership abilities in various students, including myself. She didn't just tell you what to do or what to think; she asked you questions and helped you find the answers for yourself. She believed you had it in you to problem solve and go higher.

You see, people will often live up to the expectations you place on them. I had a social studies teacher in junior high that I liked, and I felt he liked me too. But one day I made a foolish decision with some friends of mine and got in trouble. That teacher never treated me the same. From that point on, he would hardly look at me and was sharp when he spoke. He made a judgment based on his lack of approval of my behavior. When he did this, he completely lost sight of my potential.

I felt shamed and began to lose a sense of self-worth. I respected this teacher and when he no longer appeared to value me, his attitude had a negative impact on my life. Young people have a very fragile sense of self-worth. It is important as parents and teachers that we discipline negative behaviors but always continue to show value for the person. Young and old alike need to know the answer to this question. *"If I fail you, will you still love me? Will you still believe in me?"*

The choir teacher I spoke of did just the opposite of my Social Studies teacher. My choir teacher refused to believe you if you said things like, *"I can't"* or *"I am not good enough."* She would say, *"I did not hear you. Sorry, now go ahead with the piece of music I just gave you."* Thank God for people like my choir teacher.

I want to walk in honor with the people the Lord has placed in my life. I want to enjoy highlighting the good traits in others and encourage them to go higher than they ever thought they could. While Jesus walked this life, He frequently demonstrated His love for the unlovable.

Remember the woman caught in adultery? Those that gathered around were ready to condemn her. Jesus never did. Rather, after telling her He did not condemn her, He simply admonished her to go and sin no more.

Imagine how you would feel if you were that woman? Gratitude? Free? Humbled? I think she began her life anew. Jesus believed she was valuable and worthy of life. I imagine she began the long journey of healing her wounded soul as hope arose in her heart.

God's Love is...

In I Corinthians 13, we are given a full view of what love looks like through word descriptions. We also see what love is not. God's love is pure. It has no conditions.

> *1 John 4:8 "Whoever does not love does not know God, because God is love."*

Allow me to paint a word picture for you. Imagine a waterfall of pure, clear, clean water tumbling down over the rocks. The water falls into a pool that is so clear you can see the bottom. There is no sediment floating in the water. This water is crystal clear. This is the picture I have in my mind of what prophecy from God's heart would look like. Prophesy from a pure stream coming down from heaven into a pool that is clear and clean. This pool is ready for the thirsty to drink.

I was recently at a prayer meeting when I asked for prayer. I shared the title of this book with the prayer group and a gentleman immediately had a vision almost exactly as I just described. It was confirming that this is God's heart for His children, that we move in revelatory gifts in confidence and purity.

When you understand how much our Heavenly Father loves you, you are filled with so much of His goodness. But if you do not understand how He loves you, you may be prone to the "love is not" portion of the scripture.

> *1 Corinthians 13 "If I speak in the tongues of men or of angels, but do not have love, I am only a resounding gong or a clanging cymbal. If I have the gift of prophecy and can fathom all mysteries and all knowledge, and if I have a faith that can move mountains, but do not have love, I am nothing. If I give all I possess to the poor and give over my body to hardship that I may boast, but do not have love, I gain nothing.*
>
> *Love is patient, love is kind. It does not envy, it does not boast, it is not proud. It does not dishonor others, it is not self-seeking, it is not easily angered, it keeps no record of wrongs. Love does not delight in evil but rejoices with the truth. It always protects, always trusts, always hopes, always perseveres.*
>
> *Love never fails. But where there are prophecies, they will cease; where there are tongues, they will be stilled; where there is knowledge, it will pass away. For we know in part and we prophesy in part, but when completeness comes, what is in part disappears.*
>
> *When I was a child, I talked like a child, I thought like a child, I reasoned like a child. When I became a man, I put the ways of childhood behind me. For now, we see only a reflection as in a mirror; then we shall see face to face. Now I know in part; then I shall know fully, even as I am fully*

known. And now these three remain: faith, hope and love.
But the greatest of these is love."

During my lifetime, I have had many encounters with God's love. One in particular comes to mind: A family member and I had spoken sharp words to one another. Their words to me were very hurtful.

As I cried before the Lord, with my heart severely wounded, I asked Him, *"Why does it hurt so much?"*

I heard the Lord say, *"It is because you do not know how loved you really are."*

At that moment, I understood what God was saying. I needed a full revelation of His love. This surprised me, because I have known the Lord since I was a little girl. But I was in great pain, in need of my Heavenly Father's love.

I was overwhelmed by the thought and I allowed myself to get quiet and receive God's outpouring of love. I sat on my bed slowly breathing in and out with intentionality, waiting to receive a revelation. I thanked Him for His great love for me until His peace washed my soul and I knew something had changed. I grew in love that day.

Since then, the hurtful words that any person may speak against me no longer hurt like they would have in the past. The person who seemed to hurt me often with their words, began to change too. Their harsh words became fewer and far between until now negative comments are rarely spoken. Our growth releases others to grow also. This is amazing to me. Remember, there is no mud in love. Thank You, Jesus.

Activation Prayer:

Heavenly Father, thank You for Your great love that endures forever. We celebrate and rejoice in Your goodness, Lord. Jesus, would You show me how loved I am? I know what the Bible says in John 3:16; but Jesus, can You personalize this for me? As Paul says, help me to understand or comprehend how deep, how wide is the love You have for me. I want to know Your love so I can be love to other people. In Jesus' name. Amen.

Section Two

REMOVING ROADBLOCKS

Chapter Six

MINDSETS

Strongholds in Thinking

A stronghold of thought is generally a negative pattern of thinking that may have been with you most of your life.

> *2 Corinthians 10:4-5 "The weapons we fight with are not the weapons of the world. On the contrary, they have divine power to demolish strongholds. We demolish arguments and every pretension that sets itself up against the knowledge of God, and we take captive every thought to make it obedient to Christ."*

Have you ever been driving while it is snowing outside? I sure have. I have lived in the beautiful Northwest my whole life. When driving in the snow, you have to be very careful because it is hard to see the road clearly. The falling snow affects your vision. Additionally, if the roads have not been sanded or plowed, you may need to pray as you navigate your way to your destination. It is important to be prepared if you know you will be driving in the snow. Snow tires or chains should be ready to use if necessary.

I was a passenger the first time we landed in a ditch due to snowy road conditions. Being stuck in the ditch was not fun. Our tires would spin and spin, but we didn't move. Needless to say, I was praying with fervor in this situation. Getting free did take a lot of teamwork and careful strategizing. Thank the Lord, the two times this happened, we were finally able to get out of the ditch without calling a tow truck.

I use this example of driving in the snow and landing in the ditch as a word picture for what can happen when you are stuck in an old mindset. A negative mindset can get you stuck in a pattern of thinking and, like the car in the ditch, you keep spinning in one place and end up going nowhere.

Fear is a very common stronghold that many of us can relate to. Think about the fear of giving a book report or speech in school. Fear can get a grip on you and it does not let go easily unless you understand the power of agreement. For example, how do you know you are in agreement with a stronghold of fear? When fear holds you back from doing what God has called you to do or asked you to do, you are agreeing that fear is stronger than you or God.

If you want to move forward, you must renounce fear and come out of agreement with it. Break off the lies from the enemy. Then proclaim out loud that you can do whatever God has called you to do. Say out loud that you do not and will not agree with any of the lies, nor continue to remain stuck in a cycle or pattern of negativity.

I remember a time when I was in my early thirties. I was a young mother of four with a heart to worship Jesus. My husband and I had led worship together many times, and I felt "safe" worshiping with him. However, I always wanted him to lead, never leading myself. I told him I was his sidekick or backup singer and was comfortable with this arrangement.

In reality, no one knew that I was crippled with fear. The very thought of putting a microphone in my hand and singing in front of the church by myself, especially without my husband, would cause my heart to palpitate. There was no way I would ever agree to lead worship by myself. Well, God was about to set me up for an upgrade.

One Sunday morning at church a gentleman who was seated in front of me during a worship time, heard my voice and asked me if I would sing a song in their Christmas program. He explained what he had in mind for the program and felt the song was a perfect fit for my voice. *What?* Heart pounding thoughts racing through my mind. He continued stating that I had the vocal quality the song needed. I felt instant fear, then a little encouraged. Reluctantly, I said, "Yes." Well, I knew this would be the beginning of sleepless nights until that program was over.

The evening of the Christmas event arrived, and it was my turn to sing on the stage. This was not singing with the choir or my husband, this was a solo. *"Oh, here we go,"* I said to myself and quickly prayed, *"Jesus I am not doing this if You are not with me."* I remembered Moses had said that very same thing to the Lord, so I figured I was in good company.

The music director handed me the microphone as the piano started and I could not stop shaking. Both my hands and legs were trembling. I wondered to myself if everyone could see the shaking. The entire time from beginning to end, I could not stop trembling. In my mind, I was sure I must have sounded like Tiny Tim. You would have to be middle aged or older to know who he is. He was a singer in the 1960 's. The song I was thinking of was *'Tiptoe Through the Tulips.'* He was known as a performer with a quivery quality to his voice, but that was not what I was going for.

After I finished singing *'Lo How A Rose Er Blooming,'* with my trembling legs, I walked the long distance down the steps of the stage to my seat beside my husband and children. At least, it felt like a long distance. In reality, it was a short distance because we were sitting in the front row. My husband squeezed my knee and said, *"That was absolutely beautiful."* I replied, *"No it was terrible, and I will never do that again."*

I didn't know it then, but I had just made a vow by saying, *"I will never do that again."* I heard the Lord break through my thoughts and say, *"You will do it again, and again, and again. You will overcome fear."*

After heading home and getting the kids to bed, I crawled into bed with a sigh. *"It's over"* I thought to myself. Then my husband had to get all prophetic on me and told me he was hearing the Lord on my behalf. I asked him to explain. He said, *"You are seeing yourself as a grasshopper when the Lord sees you as powerful and capable."*

Wow! That hit the mark. I knew it was true. I got out of bed to lie on my face before the Lord and repent. Before I lay on the floor, I opened the Bible and it fell open to the story that my husband had just given me. Now, mind you, I had not read this portion of scripture in a long time. There was no bookmark in place. It just opened to the page. Now the tears started flowing as I read this scripture with a humble heart:

> *Numbers 13:32-34 "And they spread among the Israelites a bad report about the land they had explored. They said, "The land we explored devours those living in it. All the people we saw there are of great size. We saw the Nephilim there (the descendants of Anak come from the Nephilim). We seemed*

*like grasshoppers in our own eyes, and we looked the same
to them."*

God always has a way of confirming His Word. With tears in my eyes,
I asked the Lord to deliver me from fear and to give me eyes to see as
He sees. I so wanted to see myself as He sees me. The Lord sent me a
great peace assuring me He was pleased with my prayer.

The rest of the story was walked out through the pages of my life
in obedience and trust. I have not been perfect, but I have moved
forward to overcome fear. Every step I took was a step of faith. I
knew that the Lord would not ask me to do anything that He would
not equip me for. I grew in faith that the Lord indeed would be with
me wherever I went. And whatever He sent me to do, I would do
knowing He would anoint me with His presence as I went forward
and I would indeed succeed.

> *Isaiah 30:15 "This is what the Sovereign LORD, the Holy
> One of Israel, says: 'In repentance and rest is your salvation,
> in quietness and trust is your strength.'"*

I allowed the stronghold of fear to bow before the Lord and began
renewing my mind which is what true repentance looks like.

> *1 John 4:18 "There is no fear in love. But perfect love drives
> out fear, because fear has to do with punishment. The one
> who fears is not made perfect in love."*

Independent Spirit

The word "independent" has a positive and a negative connotation.
If you were living in a nation with a dictatorship, to become an
independent nation out from under that dictatorship would be
considered a good thing. For instance, the United States of America

has a Declaration of Independence which is a good thing. We needed freedom to be our own country and freedom to worship how we wanted.

There is, however, a negative side to this word "independent" as well. There is a demonic spirit that seeks to separate, divide and conquer by causing the minds of people to separate from one another. This is seen in families and in our churches today.

If husbands and wives make decisions on a regular basis without consideration of their spouse, an independent spirit is in operation. I am talking about small decisions and big decisions. A healthy marriage has agreement as one of its core values. In saying this, I am not taking away the headship of the husband in the home. I am saying without unity and agreement in your marriage, there will be trouble.

If a person is being oppressed by the enemy, there will probably be more than one demonic spirit at work. The enemy watches the ways of God. Let's not forget Satan once wanted to be God and still does. He understands the power of agreement and that a threefold cord is not easily broken. This principle is laid out in Ecclesiastes by King Solomon.

> *Ecclesiastes 4:9-12 "Two are better than one, because they have a good return for their labor: If either of them falls down, one can help the other up. But pity anyone who falls and has no one to help them up. Also, if two lie down together, they will keep warm. But how can one keep warm alone? Though one may be overpowered, two can defend themselves. A cord of three strands is not quickly broken."*

The Bible has many examples of laws that will happen naturally. I am not speaking of legalism but laws that are not moveable that were put in place by the Creator. For example, our Creator formed the law of gravity. It is a principle that cannot be denied. The same is true for other principles or laws such as the law of sowing and reaping. If you sow negative seeds, you will reap a negative crop and if you sow good seeds, you will reap a crop from the good you have sown. The enemy knows this, and he will also follow these laws to implement his evil purposes. The enemy will always send out two or three demons (three-fold cord) to bring the needed reinforcements to keep people in bondage.

An independent spirit often takes root due to mistrust. Mistrust takes root due to multiple disappointments. This can become a cycle through circumstances beyond our control. Without the help of the Holy Spirit, we can begin to believe the lies of the enemy as he fills our minds with thoughts that draw us into captivity. This is not what our God has for us. God has life, liberty and freedom.

If you are a little child and your parents make promises to you repeatedly, but they do not follow through, mistrust develops. This thought process which began with your parents will continue to flow over into other relationships throughout your life if not dealt with.

As a child you may have "learned" people do not mean what they say. This can lead to other thoughts such as *"If I want something done, I will have to do it myself."* This is an inner vow. If you're not careful, the enemy will try to convince you that you don't need anyone, which is the opposite of God's kingdom plan for his children. Frank Sinatra sang, *I Did It My Way.* Great song, but in the Kingdom of God, surrender and trust in Him is important, not simply, doing it our way. An independent spirit is the opposite of a surrendered heart. The Body of Christ has many members and we need each one. We are interdependent on one another.

When I was a child, I experienced multiple disappointments. My parents divorced, remarried and divorced again. We lived in poverty without a stable family life. My grandparents chose to live in a single wide trailer, so they were able to help their daughters and their children financially. I thank the Lord for my grandparents and their sacrifice of love. I will be forever grateful for the love and stability they both brought into our lives.

But even my grandparents' provision did not stop the hardships I would face as a teenager and a young woman. I experienced rape more than once by men I should have been able to trust. The effects of these horrible experiences created a root of mistrust in my heart toward men in general. As a young Christian woman, I had a conflict inside of me. I wanted to be married but at the same time, I didn't want to need a man for anything. An independent spirit had taken root through my pain. This was something I gradually became aware of and I realized I needed the Lord's help.

I loved the Lord so much and my desire was to be as close to His heart as I possibly could. I cried out for His help and deliverance. I cried out for His healing touch to mend every broken place in me. I yielded and surrendered to His Word. The Lord had to deal with my heart as He brought me into forgiveness for the men who had hurt me. I forgave the adults in my life that had let me down and for all their broken promises. I forgave those who had not protected me in the way that I needed them to. I forgave God. I forgave myself.

I am so thankful for God's Word and healing power. He transformed my mind. Together we pulled down strongholds embedded in my thoughts. This took time. In fact, it took a few years to walk through a healing process with Jesus. I would have missed out on marriage and having children had I not chosen to trust the Lord.

My husband and I are a team. We work together in building our family and on building the Kingdom. We each have our roles and lean on each other to fulfill them. A three-fold cord is not easily broken. Jesus is that third strand in our cord that keeps us together.

Rebellion

Rebellion is another one of those words that is mostly seen as negative but in some cases is necessary to bring needed change and reformation to any area. Martin Luther brought reformation to the church. In order to do this, he had to rebel against the doctrine of the church at that time. Martin Luther had a revelation as the scriptures began to unfold and understanding of the power of grace brought forth the need to be a voice for change.

Martin Luther King, Jr. did the same thing in bringing reformation to our culture and mindset in the United States of America. It was past time for equality for all, no matter the color of your skin. Thank God for reformers.

However, rebellion against God is nothing like that and is not to be taken lightly. This is a doorway that the enemy will use to walk right into your life. Satan has owned this door ever since he and a third of the angels rebelled against the Lord a long time ago. Satan wanted to be God. He wanted the worship to be directed to him and still does to this day. Personally, I want nothing to do with the enemy and his ways. But the fact is, we can participate in the sin of rebellion against God without realizing what we are doing. Thank the Lord for the blood of Jesus and the power of the mercy seat that God has established for us. Jesus' blood cleanses all negative mindsets.

From childhood, our parents work with us to learn the importance of obedience. I remember my mom telling me that any discipline I received from her was really her showing love for me, so that I would grow up to be a wonderful young woman. At the time I was sure it was some sort of a parental conspiracy, but later I understood. She wanted me to be capable of following rules that were set in place for my good, not my harm. Later, I learned from the Lord that God's rules are there to protect us. When I read the Ten Commandments,[1] I see every one of the commandments is for our good.

Young or old, sometimes the obedience pill is hard to swallow because we want to do this or that which is contrary to our parents' rules. We moan *"Why?"* to our parents if we are still living under their roof. Their rules or timeline restrictions may seem unfair. But all of this is building our character for our future.

Let's imagine a young boy whom we will call Johnny. Johnny is getting ready for school and is not in a very cooperative mood. Johnny's mom is trying her best to get him to wear his jacket before he leaves the house. She knows it is going to be cold and possibly rain soon, but Johnny refuses to wear his coat.

His mom finally gives up and lets him head out the door to school. Later, when Johnny is walking home and it is cold and wet, do you think he is a happy little boy or a cold, wet perhaps miserable boy? I imagine he may be thinking as he is walking home from school, *"I wish I would have listened to my mom and wore my coat."*

I wonder if you have had a moment similar to Johnny's, where you were told to do a certain thing like follow the speed limit sign. You choose to ignore the rule of law and now you must pay for a big fat ticket. I know I sure have. Rebellion has a price tag. We pay now or we may pay later but pay we will.

My husband and I were in a tough situation several years ago during a church plant. There were many things going on there that were hurtful to the sheep and simply wrong. God was speaking to us that we needed to leave. When we went to tell the elders of the church of our decision, we were told we were being selfish.

We ended up staying and suffered greatly. We realized later that obeying the Lord was better than the sacrifice of staying where we weren't supposed to be. It wasn't a willful rebellion, but it was disobedience. We listened to man instead of the prompting of the Lord. We repented for disobedience and finally left the situation. We were relieved. We grew a lot from that experience. Not even our mistakes are wasted in God's kingdom. Nothing at all is wasted. He will use even the hardships to mature us.

> *Deuteronomy 28:1-19 "If you fully obey the Lord your God and carefully follow all his commands I give you today, the Lord your God will set you high above all the nations on Earth. All these blessings will come on you and accompany you if you obey the Lord your God:*
>
> *You will be blessed in the city and blessed in the country. The fruit of your womb will be blessed, and the crops of your land and the young of your livestock—the calves of your herds and the lambs of your flocks. Your basket and your kneading trough will be blessed. You will be blessed when you come in and blessed when you go out.*
>
> *The Lord will grant that the enemies who rise up against you will be defeated before you. They will come at you from one direction but flee from you in seven. The Lord will send a blessing on your barns and on everything you put your hand to. The Lord your God will bless you in the land he is giving you.*

The Lord will establish you as his holy people, as he promised you on oath, if you keep the commands of the Lord your God and walk in obedience to him. Then all the people on Earth will see that you are called by the name of the Lord, and they will fear you. The Lord will grant you abundant prosperity—in the fruit of your womb, the young of your livestock and the crops of your ground—in the land he swore to your ancestors to give you.

The Lord will open the heavens, the storehouse of his bounty, to send rain on your land in season and to bless all the work of your hands. You will lend to many nations but will borrow from none. The Lord will make you the head, not the tail. If you pay attention to the commands of the Lord your God that I give you this day and carefully follow them, you will always be at the top, never at the bottom. Do not turn aside from any of the commands I give you today, to the right or to the left, following other gods and serving them."

The curses for disobedience (or rebellion);

"However, if you do not obey the Lord your God and do not carefully follow all his commands and decrees I am giving you today, all these curses will come on you and overtake you: You will be cursed in the city and cursed in the country. Your basket and your kneading trough will be cursed.

The fruit of your womb will be cursed, and the crops of your land, and the calves of your herds and the lambs of your flocks. You will be cursed when you come in and cursed when you go out, but no one will buy you."

Activation Prayer:

Heavenly Father, we humble ourselves before You and ask for forgiveness for any rebellion against your word. I choose to repent of self-centeredness and narrow thinking and ask You to renew my mindsets. The Word of God says I have the mind of Christ and I speak this over myself in the name of Jesus. Cleanse me from all rebellion, witchcraft and idolatry. Cleanse my bloodlines where the door to rebellion against You was opened. I ask that door to be shut in my bloodline and in my life. I thank You for doing this and for giving me a fresh clean start today as the roadblocks are removed. In Jesus' name. Amen.

Witchcraft

I am going to briefly touch on the subject of witchcraft, as this is one of the roadblocks people may not be aware of. A "roadblock," as it pertains to a pure stream, is defined as listed in Merriam Webster's Dictionary. It is a *"barricade often with traps or mines for holding up an enemy at a point on a road covered by fire…something that blocks progress or prevents accomplishment of an objective."*[2]

The bottom line is a roadblock which will stop or limit your progress in reaching your destination. Do you want clear communication between you and God? Do you want to receive pure words from the Lord that are not polluted? If so, you need to renounce and remove all witchcraft from your life. We want to ask the Holy Spirit to help us remove all roadblocks. Just one look at the word "witchcraft" can cause some of you to think, *"I don't know if I want to read this part of the book."* But it is important to know the enemy's tactics so you can defeat him. I remember Paul speaking about this in 2 Corinthians 2:11 *"In order that Satan might not outwit us. For we are not unaware of his schemes."*

> *1 Samuel 15:23 "For rebellion is like the sin of divination, and arrogance like the evil of idolatry. Because you have rejected the word of the Lord, he has rejected you as king."*

To rebel or participate in witchcraft is likened unto listening and obeying a different voice. Simply put, witchcraft is when we try to get answers or power apart from God or are trying to live this life apart from God relying on ourselves or others for our source of strength. This is why I believe the Lord compared witchcraft and rebellion in his Word. In the Bible story about Saul, we find a reluctant young man who is anointed to be king. He seems sincere at first glance, but unfortunately, he fell into demonic oppression and sin through rebellion and idolatry and he even participated in witchcraft. [3]

The story of King Saul is epic indeed. There is power, plot and attempted murder surrounding this King who was once anointed by God through the prophet Samuel. Sadly, Saul later turns away from God to self-idolatry and witchcraft. Saul knew what God told him to do, but rather he feared the disapproval of men more than God. Often the same is true with many of us. Deep down, we know what we are supposed to do, but we deceive ourselves by pretending we are doing right.

The good news is because of Jesus' blood, we can ask for forgiveness and it will be freely given to us. In the case of Saul, I believe the Lord God knew what was in Saul's heart and how Saul would continue to rule as a king full of anger, competition, and greed. The Lord saw that Saul's heart was more for himself than obeying the Lord. This is why the Lord was grieved that He had made Saul the king.

Witchcraft can come in different forms. Many times, people will go to psychics or tarot card readers for their answers instead of God. They do not realize that they have opened the door to demonic influence in their lives. Some examples include but are not limited to: Ouija boards, mediums, horoscopes, or anything else that can be used to get answers. Basically, any other source but God. Saul himself committed this sin by going to the witch of Endor to call up the spirit of Samuel. (See 1 Samuel 28.) There are two power sources, one light and one dark. Which power source do you run to? Choose carefully.

As a three-year-old child, I had given my life to Jesus. By age seven, I had discovered that I had the gift to discern spirits. Through these experiences, I learned that there was light and dark, meaning angels and demons. The enemy used to frighten me with the things I would "see". It was frightening at a young age, to have this gift and no one to train me how to use it. I do believe that most children are more sensitive to the spirit world than many adults.

We need to train our children about the angels of the Lord and how many there are compared to the fallen angels that have turned away from God (demons). Share with your children that both types of angels have power, but God's power always triumphs. We can emphasize that the almighty God has two thirds more angels than the enemy has demons. The enemy may roar like a lion but God thunders from heaven. This will empower your children to see our God for who He is. Big God— little devil. The name of Jesus will chase the demons away.

Unfortunately, there is witchcraft in the church that many are unaware of. This type comes in the form of manipulation, control, seduction, flattery and intimidation. With this type of witchcraft, you will not see a witch flying around like in storybooks, spells or incantations. However, this is real, and the effects have the capacity to take your peace and manipulate your emotions.

Many who are in the churches today have said the sinner's prayer, yet inside, they are not truly free. The struggle with jealousy in their hearts is real and often you will find these believers doing many acts of service to gain attention from the leadership rather than having the motive to simply please the Lord by serving others. As Jesus said, *"Be careful not to practice your righteousness in front of others to be seen by them. If you do, you will have no reward from your Father in Heaven"* (Matthew 6:1).

Jesus knew the potential traps the enemy would lay. The enemy wants to get people focused on themselves rather than focused on God. If the enemy cannot take away your faith, he will try to keep manipulating you like his puppet. His seductive lies tell you exactly what your flesh wants to hear.

When a person is under the influence of witchcraft, often they will flatter you with compliments and act as if they want to be your best friend in the beginning. Yet behind closed doors, they speak against you. When they pray for you, it is a prayer of manipulation for what they want to happen in your life rather than being led by the Holy Spirit of God.

Whole books have been written on this topic, as well as articles found in various magazines such as *Charisma*. Many of these books deal with what is called the Jezebel spirit. Some of these books are very helpful and others I feel leave the reader with a mindset to label someone as having the spirit of Jezebel just because they have a strong leadership gift. Please be careful to first inspect your own fruit rather than everyone else's.

I do want to leave you with a list of symptoms you may be experiencing if someone in your world is operating or being influenced by a spirit of witchcraft. These symptoms come straight from the Bible. I first gained understanding on the effects of word curses and witchcraft through Rick Joiners book, 'Overcoming Witchcraft.'[4] If you read his book, on pages 24-29 you will find a list similar to mine, though except for two, I used different words for descriptions of the effect of witchcraft. Here is a short list of possible effects of this evil spirit:

Discouragement
Despair for no reason
Disillusionment
Confusion
Indecisiveness
Fatigue
Weariness
Suicidal thoughts
Feeling like quitting: the ministry or your job, leaving your family
Isolation

In the Bible, we read about a mighty man of God, Elijah. After defeating the prophets of Baal through the power of God, this prophet was threatened by Jezebel through her witchcraft. This so affected his mind that he ran for his life and hid in a cave. As you read this scripture, see if you can identify the symptoms I previously listed as evidence witchcraft may be involved. Elijah lost all confidence in himself and his ability to do his assignments from the Lord.

> *1 Kings 19:1-18 "Now Ahab told Jezebel everything Elijah had done and how he had killed all the prophets with the sword. So, Jezebel sent a messenger to Elijah to say, "May the gods deal with me, be it ever so severely, if by this time tomorrow I do not make your life like that of one of them.*
>
> *Elijah was afraid and ran for his life. When he came to Beersheba in Judah, he left his servant there, while he himself went a day's journey into the wilderness. He came to a broom*

bush, sat down under it and prayed that he might die. 'I have had enough, Lord,' he said. 'Take my life; I am no better than my ancestors.' Then he lay down under the bush and fell asleep.

All at once an angel touched him and said, 'Get up and eat.' He looked around, and there by his head was some bread baked over hot coals, and a jar of water. He ate and drank and then lay down again.

The angel of the Lord came back a second time and touched him and said, 'Get up and eat, for the journey is too much for you.' So, he got up and ate and drank. Strengthened by that food, he traveled forty days and forty nights until he reached Horeb, the mountain of God. There he went into a cave and spent the night.

The Lord Appears to Elijah, and the word of the Lord came to him: 'What are you doing here, Elijah?'

He replied, 'I have been very zealous for the Lord God Almighty. The Israelites have rejected your covenant, torn down your altars, and put your prophets to death with the sword. I am the only one left, and now they are trying to kill me too.'

The Lord said, 'Go out and stand on the mountain in the presence of the Lord, for the Lord is about to pass by.'

Then a great and powerful wind tore the mountains apart and shattered the rocks before the Lord, but the Lord was not in the wind. After the wind there was an earthquake, but the Lord was not in the earthquake. After the earthquake came a fire, but the Lord was not in the fire. And after the fire came a gentle whisper. When Elijah heard it, he pulled his cloak over his face and went out and stood at the mouth of the cave.

Then a voice said to him, 'What are you doing here, Elijah?'

He replied, 'I have been very zealous for the Lord God Almighty. The Israelites have rejected your covenant, torn down your altars, and put your prophets to death with the sword. I am the only one left, and now they are trying to kill me too.'

The Lord said to him, 'Go back the way you came, and go to the Desert of Damascus. When you get there, anoint Hazael king over Aram. Also, anoint Jehu son of Nimshi king over Israel, and anoint Elisha son of Shaphat from Abel Meholah to succeed you as prophet. Jehu will put to death any who escape the sword of Hazael, and Elisha will put to death any who escape the sword of Jehu. Yet I reserve seven thousand in Israel—all whose knees have not bowed down to Baal and whose mouths have not kissed him.'"

If you read this passage of scripture carefully, you can see the strategy of the enemy at work to defeat Elijah through the power of thought. The enemy was working on Elijah's emotions or mind. But you also can see how the Lord ever so gently restores Elijah's spirit man to the truth of who he is and who his God is. Elijah needed to know he was not alone.

The enemy always likes to make us feel alone and tells us we are the only one who is struggling. It is a trick and a trap to keep you isolated. Can you identify instances when the enemy used those lies or symptoms against you?

God restores us to truth in gentleness and with great love just like he did Elijah. God sees what the enemy is doing, and He knows we are but flesh. God knows what we are called to do and so does the enemy. That is why the enemy works so hard to try and stop us from being who we are called to be.

You are a rare and valuable treasure in the hand of the Lord. There is brilliance in you that must be seen. Allow your light to shine brightly and do the part God has called you to do. Without you, there will be a piece missing and the fullness of God's plan will not be felt. Recognize the enemies' wiles and choose God's victory instead!

Take Action:

Pray a prayer of repentance with me to come out of agreement with the enemy and his lies:

Dear Heavenly Father, I thank You for Your great love for me. Thank You for Your Son, Jesus Christ my Lord and Savior and for His precious blood that cleanses me from all sin. I ask You, Jesus, to forgive me for in any way participating with the spirit of witchcraft knowingly or unknowingly. Also, forgive me for times I may have been jealous or manipulating and controlling. Forgive me and wash me now with Your cleansing blood, Jesus.

Wash me from words spoken in secret against me by another person under the influence of Jezebel and witchcraft. Remove all symptoms of despair and other demonic curses from me now in Jesus' name. I come out of agreement from the enemies' lies, traps and snares. Thank You for restoring me to a full and complete sound mind in the name of Jesus. Amen.

Chapter Seven

OUT OF THE MOUTH

Word Curses

So often we just speak our mind without giving any thought to the outcome of our words. We often take venting our emotions to the next level of negativity. This negativity can be damaging to both the one who spoke it and the one who hears it.

> *Proverbs 18:21 "The tongue has the power of life and death, and those who love it will eat its fruit."*

> *Romans 12:14 "Bless those who persecute you; bless and do not curse."*

Luke 6:27-28 "But to you who are listening I say: 'Love your enemies, do good to those who hate you, bless those who curse you, pray for those who mistreat you.'"

As you can read in the scriptures, the Lord is clear that there is power released from words of blessing or words of cursing. There is a reason the Word says to not sin in your anger.[1] Anger is an emotion that we all have. God Himself has the emotion of anger. Yet, the key is not to sin while you are angry. A question I asked the Lord years ago was, *"How can we be angry and sin not?"*

Luke 5:22 "But I tell you that anyone who is angry with a brother or sister will be subject to judgment. Again, anyone who says to a brother or sister, 'Raca,' is answerable to the court. And anyone who says, 'You fool!' will be in danger of the fire of hell."

Wow, that is a pretty intense teaching Jesus gave. When I think of the many times I have misused words in anger, I am grateful for His mercy and grace in my life. It seems Jesus wanted His followers to understand the importance of the heart condition and the power of words.

Jesus knows that the content of our hearts will be spoken out of our mouths.[2] He told the Pharisee that it is not what goes into a man that makes him unclean but what comes out of him. Jesus was trying to teach His followers to be careful of both their hearts and their words. Why do you think He would emphasize this topic in so many ways? I believe it's because He loves everyone and does not want to see others hurt through words spoken in ignorance.

Do you remember the childhood chant, *"Sticks and stones may break my bones, but names will never hurt me?"*[3] My brother and I used to say that to each other often as an empowering statement when we would disagree or try to prove we were right and the other was most certainly wrong. To prove our childish point, we would call each other names and make hurtful statements like, "*You are just stupid!*" Then our ace in the hole was to chant the poem over and over again, sometimes sticking out our tongues at each other. We really did love each other and were the best of friends most of the time.

Effects of negative words spoken against you can feel subtle at first. This is true for words you've heard someone speak and even words you did not hear them speak. Words can still affect you, even if you are unaware of their impact. For example: You are feeling good doing your thing, getting work done and then, suddenly, your emotions change like the weather. Suddenly, you are feeling down in the dumps when only moments before you had been feeling perfectly normal. You may pause and think *"What is wrong with me?"* Maybe you feel overwhelmed. Only moments before, the tasks felt doable but now seem impossible to complete.

Chances are, someone has spoken against you or the work you are doing with an organization you are affiliated with. Those words carry negative energy which can be felt. It is real. And it can come against you and affect your thinking. The words we speak can also release demonic activity into another person's life as well as our own. Like rats sniffing out garbage, our hurtful and critical words release an aroma which attract the demons.

The beautiful truth is, in the same way that word curses hurt, words of blessing will release an aroma that attracts the angels who then release the goodness of God into the lives of others. Yes, you can completely bless the other person by speaking highly of them, declaring the Word of the Lord over their life and releasing an angelic presence around them. He is amazingly wonderful.

Psalm 103:20-22 "Praise the Lord, you his angels, you mighty ones who do his bidding, who obey his word. Praise the Lord, all his heavenly hosts, you his servants who do his will. Praise the Lord, all his works everywhere in his dominion. Praise the Lord, my soul."

I remember years ago when my children were young, and we were attending a new church. We all agreed we liked the church and wanted to keep going to see if this was our place of worship and fellowship. One Sunday after attending for a few months, as we were coming in through the doors, a dark heavy feeling washed over me. It was not a good feeling.

I said to my husband, *"I can't seem to shake this feeling of rejection."*

He said he felt it too. He continued, *"I feel like leaving now, I feel completely uncomfortable and unwanted."*

I looked at my young children who had overheard their parents' discussion. As I looked at each child, they began to nod their heads. Each one said they felt the same feeling and thought leaving would be a good idea. My husband and I began to ask the Lord what this feeling was all about. The Lord began to teach us why it happened.

As we dug into the Bible, our eyes were opened regarding the power of our words. We began to understand that words bring either a positive or negative effect. In the example I shared with you regarding my family feeling rejected, we knew immediately that it was demonic and oppressive. We just wanted to know why the enemy thought he had authority to be at the church entrance in the first place.

After prayer and study, we felt certain the enemy was behind this. We believed words had been spoken in the church by folks that were hurtful or critical. These words of rejection were released into the atmosphere, which was all the enemy needed to set up that demonic assignment at the front door of the church.

The enemy does not want church growth, he does not want God's people in unity or harmony. He wants to keep us isolated and alone because he knows the threat from and strength in corporate unity. Now were these words specifically against us? I do not believe so.

My thought is that the enemy was very busy speaking lies of negativity and some folks at the church had chosen to listen to those words and release them. Maybe they felt hurt or rejected by one of the pastors and, in their hurt and anger, they grumbled at the door. I would bet that others had felt it as they walked into the building.

Often, we think we are the only one going through something, when indeed others are going through the same thing. The enemy will take out as many as he can in any given moment. I have since learned how to pray when something like that comes against me or my family.

This is what I do and recommend to others who want to cut off all word curses or words spoken against them or the will of God for their lives. First, I begin to pray that every word spoken against me, God will replace with blessings. I pray that whatever negative emotions that had been felt will leave at that moment.

If you do this, you will feel like yourself again. Take the next step to praise and worship the Lord. I guarantee you will feel empowered. Let's purpose to be those who release life into the atmosphere. Let's release life into the hearts of others, even those that speak against us. Let's love them and bless them as Jesus tells us to do in the Bible. What a mighty force the church would be on the earth if God's children really grabbed hold of this truth and lived it out. No power in hell could stand against it.

Bullying

Our words often produce our outcome. Many folks have often quoted a portion of scripture from Proverbs, *"As a man thinks in his heart, so is he."* [4] As discussed in the previous section, there are many other scriptures that talk about the importance of our thought life and our words.

I am always excited when I hear how Science is backing up the Word of God with the latest findings in many areas. The Lord knows how we are made. When Jesus walked the earth, one of His roles was as a teacher. As Jesus taught the Word, He expanded their thinking. He taught about unjust anger equaling murder, and how rash words such as 'you fool' can lead to judgment. In other words, your thoughts do matter, because they affect your heart. And your heart can affect your actions.

Here is a sampling of scripture that speaks of the power of our thoughts and words:

> *Mark 7:21 "For it is from within, out of a person's heart, that evil thoughts come—sexual immorality, theft, murder…"*

> *Proverbs 4:23 "A good man brings good things out of the good stored up in his heart, and an evil man brings evil things out of the evil stored up in his heart. For the mouth speaks what the heart is full of."*

> *Philippians 4:8 "Finally, brothers and sisters, whatever is true, whatever is noble, whatever is right, whatever is pure, whatever is lovely, whatever is admirable—if anything is excellent or praiseworthy—think about such things."*

> *Romans 12:2 "Do not conform to the pattern of this world but be transformed by the renewing of your mind. Then you*

will be able to test and approve what God's will is—his good, pleasing and perfect will."

2 Corinthians 10:3-5 "For though we live in the world, we do not wage war as the world does. The weapons we fight with are not the weapons of the world. On the contrary, they have divine power to demolish strongholds. We demolish arguments and every pretension that sets itself up against the knowledge of God, and we take captive every thought to make it obedient to Christ."

Science has proven that words do have power. There have been several studies done on this topic that have tested and proven that our words have the power of life or death.

There is a study that has captured a lot of attention which can be googled for verification and watched on YouTube™.[5] This study has gained a lot of attention through social media to help young people understand that bullying others causes great damage to the mind, will and emotions. Many teachers and social workers contributed that, in certain cases, the bullying led to attempted or completed suicide.

In hopes of educating children and adults concerning the danger of bullying, IKEA™, a worldwide merchant out of Sweden decided to conduct their own study and test the effects of negative and positive words. IKEA teamed up with the G.E.M.S. schools. The G.E.M.S. schools are an international private education program with its headquarters in Dubai.[6] These schools are located in many nations. A few mentioned included: The United Kingdom, United States, Singapore, India, Saudi Arabia, Qatar, Egypt, Kenya, Switzerland and the United Arab Emirates.

The test stations consisted of two large potted plants, set up a few feet apart. The plants were surrounded with a clear plastic-glass looking encasing. Each plant received the same amount of water and sunlight. The plants were potted with the same soil. The only difference was one plant had a sign in front of it to receive words of kindness or compliments and the other plant had a sign saying this plant is to be bullied with negative harsh words.

Words of encouragement were spoken throughout the day such as, *"You are important," "You are smart,"* or *"You will be very successful."* The bullied plant did not fare so well. This plant received harsh words spoken to it daily; several times a day. Words like *"You are a stupid idiot"* or *"You will never amount to anything."*

Teachers even recorded the words of students in class speaking to the plant with complements or words to reinforce the bullying and they would play these recordings to the appropriate plant. An important component to remember when you see the results of these tests is that both plants received the *exact amount of water, sunshine and fertilizer.* The soil was the *same.* The only difference between the two plants, was the words being spoken. The outcome of this experiment was revealing indeed and has been seen worldwide through the technology of social media.

As you may have guessed, the plant that received the words of encouragement thrived. The leaves were green, and the plant looked completely healthy. The plant that received hateful words looked as if it were dying. It drooped and the leaves were turning brown. The experiment was successful in teaching children that bullying is serious business.

I saw several experiments on YouTube™ where others conducted and recorded their own experiments similar to IKEA. Funny thing, the same thing happened over and over again. Words of life brought life to the plants and words of death brought death.

A Japanese researcher Dr. Masaru Emoto's conducted similar experiments with water and rice.[7] His research revealed that the vibrations from words and thoughts will affect the molecular structure of water. Dr. Emoto has spoken on this topic around the world. He has written several books that educate people on the power of words.

It is general knowledge that the human body is made up of a great deal of water. For instance, a young child's body composition is upwards of 95 percent water. By the time we reach adulthood the amount decreases to 70 percent. It is the same amount of water on the earth. The water content in trees varies between 50 to 90 percent.

Dr. Emoto wanted to find out what would happen when he froze a droplet of water into ice crystals on a slide, while testing the difference between positive and negative energy frequency. The frequencies were in the form of different sounds like music, or words spoken as the water froze on a slide or container.

Dr. Emoto froze samples of water from many different locations. and examined them under a microscope to compare the form of each droplet. They were beautiful and each one different. He then experimented with sound. He chose music samples. Some were classical like Bach or Beethoven. In contrast, he compared the sound and music as he played heavy metal. The ice crystal from classical music formed beautiful crystals. But, in my opinion, the heavy metal music ice crystals looked distressed.

He also experimented with different spoken words to see what would happen. The results were amazing. Words like hate or kill formed darker crystals with little form to them. They even might be considered scary looking. In contrast, words spoken of hope or peace looked like a snowflake with an array of beauty.

Taking it a step further, he experimented with rice and water. He took three jars and separated them several inches. In one jar he spoke *"Thank you"* to the other he said, *"You're an idiot,"* and the third he wrote *"Ignored."* After thirty days, the one he spoke *"Thank you"* to, began to bubble with a nice fermentation and fragrance. The one with the words *"You're an idiot,"* turned black, and the rice that was ignored began to rot. This is an important lesson to the power of the spoken word.

Many have called Dr. Emoto's work pseudo-science, meaning it is not recognized by the scientific community at large. And yet others see the work as having great scientific value. You can decide for yourself.

A woman I greatly respect is Dr. Carolyn Leaf, whose scientific research on our thoughts, words and the brain have been recognized and documented. She has written several books on this subject with scientific backing.[8] If you can study any of her books, DVD's or CD's, you will be blown away with the amount of scripture and science she has woven together. She is one of my personal favorites on the subject of the brain, the mind and our words. Please check out her materials. They are life changing.

No wonder God lets us know there is life and death in the power of our tongue. Judge for yourselves. Plants have a cellular structure and they contain water. Creation is made by God and has a cellular structure. Water is in every living thing.

We see this in the Bible when Jesus spoke to a fig tree and cursed it.[9] When seen later, it had withered. That is an example of the power in your words. Jesus also spoke life and people were healed or raised from the dead. If I have a question with any topic or concern, I just open my Bible and read about Jesus. I find my answers. *What was Jesus doing? What was Jesus saying?* In following Jesus, we are led to the life-giving power in His very name. Jesus.

When I was afraid as a child, I would sing a beautiful song over myself about the name of Jesus and peace always washed over my soul. This song was my weapon against fear. The words spoke peace and trust to my soul. It was called 'There's Just Something About That Name' by Bill and Gloria Gaither. Please go to YouTube™ and listen to this beautiful song.[17] It is so very soothing and comforting.

Change Your Words, Change Your Life

Romans 10:17 (KJV) "So then faith cometh by hearing, and hearing by the word of God."

If you believe the Word of God is true, then it stands to reason that we need to speak the Word of God over our lives and circumstances. Why? Because the Word of God will cause our faith to grow. The Bible teaches that the Word of God is living and active.

Hebrews 4:12 "For the word of God is alive and active. Sharper than any double-edged sword, it penetrates even to dividing soul and spirit, joints and marrow; it judges the thoughts and attitudes of the heart."

God's Word is living. His Word is alive!

John 1:14 "The Word became flesh and made his dwelling among us. We have seen his glory, the glory of the one and only Son, who came from the Father, full of grace and truth."

The Bible teaches in Genesis 1:1-27 that God created the heavens and the earth. He created light and darkness. God created everything that lives and breathes and walks the earth. He did it all through His spoken word. He used words to create all the beauty we enjoy now.

Genesis 1:27 "So God created mankind in his own image, in the image of God he created them; male and female he created them."

Since we are created in God's image and He is the Creator, we can create also. We get to create or change our atmospheres by speaking the Word of God. If your home feels chaotic and family members are quarreling, speak peace into the atmosphere. Begin to worship God in that atmosphere and watch it change.

If we speak life into another person with words of encouragement, we will see the results of our words almost immediately. As hope arises in their hearts, their countenance also changes. Those words of encouragement you speak foster the growth of hope. Hope is an ingredient desperately needed in the world today.

I cannot tell you how many times I've been at the grocery store check-out line and been thanked by the cashier for making their day. I would simply speak positive words to the person ringing up my groceries. Even at restaurants, waiters have told my husband and I how nice it is to wait on someone who is cheerful and thankful. Sometimes we are able to bless our waiter/waitress with a prayer and prophetic word before we are finished with our meal.

How wonderful to know that you can be an agent of change in someone else's life. Jesus said we are the light of the world. As believers, we have the opportunity to bring light into dark places. The number one way we do this is by the spoken word. It's really a miracle to truly understand the fact that by speaking the word God places on your heart to another human being, you have the opportunity to create life for that person.

As a young believer, I was challenged to change my self-talk. I noticed how very little I believed in myself. I allowed the hardships of life to beat me down. Words others had spoken against me had taken root in my soul and a silent pain deep inside was always present. I thought of going to college but then would talk myself out of it. I would tell myself things like, *"You'd have to do math and you are terrible at math."* I was afraid to apply for certain jobs because I just knew the chances of getting the job were slim to none. So why try? People, this is no way to live. Jesus said He has given us life more abundantly.

> *John 10:10 "The thief comes only to steal and kill and destroy;*
> *I have come that they may have life, and have it to the full."*

What I was experiencing was not life in the way Jesus said it should be. I was tired of living this way. I was only nineteen years old. I thought, *"My goodness! I need help, this has got to stop."* Every time the negative voices would speak in my head, I began to counter the negative and would speak the truth of God's Word.

This was like Jesus when He was led into the wilderness to be tempted by the devil. The enemy twisted the truth and Jesus spoke back to the enemy with the actual truth of the Word of God. Listening to the dialog in our mind, we can forget we have an enemy. The enemy does not want us to know who we are in Christ and what we can do. He is terrified for us to grab scriptures like:

> *Philippians 4:13 "I can do all this through him who gives*
> *me strength."*

Speaking words over ourselves that are encouraging to our souls will help us as we press on toward our goals, despite the hardships that may be surrounding us. We must establish that God's Word is true and come into agreement with it. Remember God's Word is living and active and life and death are in the power of the tongue. As we speak life into our circumstances with expectancy, positive change is coming.

I have watched my own children respond to the power of words, both negatively and positively. I have seen the difference in their behavior when I speak into their destiny with words of truth and encouragement. They start to believe in themselves and therefore their capacity to excel can be seen. But, when I have nagged them to get moving to get their homework done or tell them to try harder (blah, blah), I have found those types of words had little positive effect and only brought frustration between parent and child. Simply put, nothing gets done.

However, when I encourage my children by reminding them that God created each one with purpose and intelligence, nothing is too difficult for them in Christ Jesus. When they hear from me that they can do it, there is a much better response. We need to keep this principle in mind, especially when we are prophesying. We are speaking on behalf of God.

> *1 Peter 4:11 "If anyone speaks, they should do so as one who speaks the very words of God. If anyone serves, they should do so with the strength God provides, so that in all things God may be praised through Jesus Christ. To him be the glory and the power for ever and ever. Amen."*

To ensure you have a pure stream and that your words are from heaven, you must guard your inner conversations. You must be certain that you are speaking what is positive and uplifting to yourself and others.

I have experienced people who felt that they had a word from God for me, but as they spoke, I could sense that it was not the word of the Lord, but rather something they themselves were going through. It is possible their own personal world at the time was full of negative self-talk, negative thoughts or words against others, therefore, the word released did not carry the strength or truth it could have.

Activation Prayer:

Heavenly Father, I give You my words. I give You my mind. I ask You to renew my mind with Your words and Your thoughts. Remind me to speak to others what is good. Remind me to call out the 'gold' in the person I may be frustrated with or who may have hurt me. Show me how You see each person You place in my life. Remind me, Lord, to speak over myself words that build my inner man into what You've called me to be. Lord, please show me any lies I have been believing about myself. I renounce those lies in Jesus' name. I declare that I no longer align with those lies. Lord, would You show me the truth of how You see me. I come into agreement with Your truth as I accept and receive what You say about me.

Lord, I ask You again, in Jesus' name, to break off of my life every word curse that I have spoken or has been spoken against me. Thank You for replacing every negative word with words of blessings. I release Your truth over my identity in the name of Jesus. Let me be a change agent for Your kingdom and Your glory. Amen.

Chapter Eight
HUMILITY

What Goes Before a Fall?

The Bible lets us know that Satan was one of the most beautiful angels in heaven. Out of his very being came glorious music. But as time went on, pride was found in him. Instead of being a worshiper of the creator God, he wanted to be worshiped.

> *Isaiah 14:12-14 "How you have fallen from Heaven, morning star, son of the dawn! You have been cast down to the earth, you who once laid low the nations! You said in your heart, "I will ascend to the heavens; I will raise my throne above the stars of God; I will sit enthroned on the mount of assembly, on the utmost heights of Mount Zaphon.*

I will ascend above the tops of the clouds; I will make myself like the Most High."

For further scriptural information regarding Satan's fall, read Ezekiel 28:12-17.

Most of us can say with all honesty that we have had to ask forgiveness from the Lord for walking in pride. It is a sneaky sin; often the prideful person is the last one to recognize it. *"Me? Pride? Oh nonsense."*

Proverbs 16:18 "Pride goes before destruction, a haughty spirit before a fall."

Pride, as with many English words, has a double meaning. For instance, it is good to take pride in your work. When you know you worked hard on that project and have done your personal best, or when you have stepped up your workout routine and have finally lost those last ten pounds that have hung on forever. Good for you. You should be proud of yourself for achieving your goals.

When a person is walking in pride, the unhealthy kind, you will notice they have a need to always be right. They must win any argument or discussion. The need to be right is more important to them than the relationships they are in. It matters not that their need to be right is hurting someone else. They desire to be seen and known as always being right. The need to be right is usually rooted in deep insecurity often due to traumatic childhood events. Jesus was the most righteous person to ever walk the planet. Yet, He did not need to argue or fight to be right (correct). What mattered to Jesus was his right standing with His Heavenly Father. Knowing that was enough.

In the entertainment industry, we have seen a scenario play out over and over again. The entertainer starts out humbly and excited, but if quickly propelled into the limelight of fame, over time, many succumb to a prideful mindset. This can happen in any industry that comes with being the top dog or gaining a lot of notoriety. The Christian community is not immune to this sneaky foe either. Many pastors and conference speakers who become popular and well known can stumble with pride. They begin to see themselves above others, abuse this newfound power and end up hurting others. This makes it tough on marriages as well. We need to remember to pray for those who are in the limelight.

While my husband and I worked in a marriage ministry, we saw many marriages healed and restored. The times when we did not, there were two issues in one or both of the involved parties that were most commonly blocking them: pride and unforgiveness. Either the husband or wife was not willing to forgive and to admit that they could have been wrong. Sometimes, there was an unwillingness to see the pain their actions had brought to their spouse.

Without humility and the willingness to forgive, couples do not last long. It is hard to witness a marriage heading for a divorce. If one or the other spouse chooses themselves (pride) over their marriage partner, with whom they had exchanged vows as they made a covenant before God and man, the marriage does not last. Tragically, the children suffer the effects of their parents' hard hearts for years to come.

Having said all this, there are times when a divorce is necessary such as in cases of abuse (verbal or physical) or sexual misconduct (adultery). In those cases, usually professional help is needed, as well as deliverance and inner healing. But remember, there is nothing too difficult for our God. If a person will humble themselves, any problem can be overcome.

Activation Prayer:

Heavenly Father, thank You for loving me unconditionally. Thank You for Jesus, Your Son, showing us the way to live. Soften my heart in the places I have hardened it through my life's disappointments. Help me to forgive and admit when I have been wrong. Forgive me as I forgive those who have hurt me. Keep me humble as I walk this life, always remembering to put others above myself. Thank You that every good and perfect gift comes from You, God, and I give You thanks and praise for all that You have given to me. In Jesus' name. Amen.

Jesus as Our Role Model

Jesus was the perfect picture of strength and humility. He was fully God and fully man.

> Colossians 2:9 "For in Christ all the fullness of the Deity lives in bodily form."

> Philippians 2:5-8 "In your relationships with one another, have the same mindset as Christ Jesus: who, being in very nature God, did not consider equality with God something to be used to his own advantage; rather, he made himself nothing by taking the very nature of a servant, being made in human likeness and being found in appearance as a man he humbled himself, by becoming obedient to death, even death on a cross!"

Humility can show itself in various ways. I have been to many conferences around the United States and even the world. I find the same issue wherever I go. People are literally running to the front to get the best seat possible. I have been pushed and almost knocked down at a Christian conference. My goodness, you would have thought it was a Black Friday event at Walmart. Unfortunately, there is something I have yet to see; someone giving up their place in the front for another.

I understand it is nice to sit in the front. You can see everything more clearly. When you are petite like me, even a person of average height can block my view. And yet, what would happen if we slowed down and enjoyed the moment, allowing others to go ahead of us? What would the world look like if we were more concerned with being a blessing instead of trying so hard to be blessed? When we are in the front, it's possible that we would have been recognized. But when we take the position in the back and honor another person, God sees and smiles upon us. The devil cannot feed on the flesh of a person who walks in humility.

There was a time when I was serving on staff at a church. I had been falsely accused of saying things against my senior leaders. I was called into a meeting with one of the pastors and an elder. That was a very dark time for me, and I was learning a lot about leadership, kingdom authority in Jesus, and the enemy. This particular evening, I was very sick with strep throat and running a fever of 102 degrees. I let them know I was sick, but they said it was important and to come anyway. In obedience, I went to the meeting. When the moment of accusation came, there was not an ounce of mercy in the room. It was very clear that they believed the negative report about me.

As I sat in my chair, I heard the voice of the Lord through the pain, hurt and the sickness. The Lord spoke to me, *"Go low."* I slid down from my chair onto the floor and stayed on my knees. I humbled myself, did not defend myself even though I could have. I simply spoke, please forgive me for anything that could have brought this about. There were tears streaming from my eyes and I was not alone. Everyone in the room began to shed tears. It was a very holy moment. You see, when you walk as Jesus walked in humility, power is released. We can fight and defend ourselves or we can allow the Lord of Hosts to be our defender. As I left the meeting that evening, I was favored by God and man.

I decided to hold a meeting with my staff of about thirty in my department. I chose to put on a pair of boots as a prophetic act. An old song ran through my mind, *'These Boots Were Made for Walking.'* Who was I going to walk on? Satan.

> *Romans 16:20 "The God of peace will soon crush Satan under your feet. The grace of our Lord Jesus be with you."*

I was determined to kick the enemy out by staying low and apologizing to the entire team for any word spoken that reflected negatively on my senior leaders. As I apologized, I kicked the air with my boots on and said, *"I am not letting the enemy get away with bringing division to this team or this church."* I proceeded to explain why I had called them to this meeting, and I asked for forgiveness as I had planned. My entire team was there minus two. The two who had accused me were not there.

Everyone said, *"You did not say those words. You did not speak against your leadership. In fact, you were very gracious as you communicated."* They continued to let me know that I had completely spoken in honor of my leadership. The group voiced the same words in different ways. I was not guilty of this accusation.

When I walked out the door with tears of joy in my eyes, my most senior leader told me, *"Tina, I believed in you the whole time…I know your heart and character and I am so very proud of you."*

If I had chosen to defend myself, which would have been easy to do, I would have presented myself in a prideful manner. So often when we jump to defend ourselves, pride and fear are doing the talking. Remember, when anyone gives prophetic words with pride in their heart, the word can very easily be polluted or tainted. But prophecy from a pure stream comes through humility before God and man.

Look at what can happen when we go low, walk in humility and allow the Lord to fight for us. People of God, this is what Jesus did time and again when he was accused. Jesus simply continued his assignment on earth, full of grace and power. Jesus now sits enthroned in the heavens. He had given up that place to come to earth, but after obedience even unto death on the cross, He received His rightful place. He is the King of Kings. Remember the devil cannot feed on the flesh of a person who walks in humility.

Activation Prayer:

Thank You, Jesus, for the power of humility. You demonstrated it for me as You did not insult those who were insulting you. You chose to stay quiet and stand strong in the confidence of who You are. No one can take that from You. Teach me to stay humble and go low as I daily encounter opportunities that test me in this. You make me strong. In Jesus' name. Amen.

How is Your Hearing?

Pride is a thief to your true self. It can hinder your ability to hear God and to hear others. Pride can distort your vision. I can even go so far as to say, pride is possibly the number one roadblock to all communication. When pride is in action, you see only what you want to see. For some reason, pride will magnify the faults in others, so you end up doing what Jesus warned you not to do.

> *Matthew 4:4-5 "How can you say to your brother, 'Let me take the speck out of your eye,' when all the time there is a plank in your own eye? You hypocrite, first take the plank out of your own eye, and then you will see clearly to remove the speck from your brother's eye."*

Get rid of pride and you will see clearly enough to help another person. How can anyone expect to receive the word of the Lord for another person when pride is present? Pride will distort the word of the Lord like nothing else. The Pharisees in Jesus' day had a religious spirit, but it was pride that they were seeped in. The Bible tells us that they had envy against Jesus and were more concerned with how many followers Jesus had then whether Jesus was speaking the truth.

> *Matthew 27:18 (KJV) "For he knew that for envy they had delivered him."*

When we are walking in pride, we cannot hear others clearly. Our focus is so much on ourselves that we literally can steamroll right over a person. If someone is actively walking in the sin of pride, you will find that if any questions are asked, or even the smallest challenge to their viewpoint is expressed, the voice of pride will respond and speak in a harsh and uncaring manner. Who can stand under someone's harsh words? We have established in the previous chapter how damaging negative words can be, and how positive and life-giving words of encouragement are.

I enjoy word pictures because they tend to stick in my mind's eye. I believe this is one reason Jesus taught in word pictures and story form. Here's a word picture for you: Pride is like a hairball in your kitchen sink. Just as the hairball clogs the pipes and keeps the water from moving through, so pride clogs the movement of the Lord in your life. Humility can be the Drano˚ in your kitchen sink. Pour a little in and that pride hairball is gone. Things then start moving as they should.

Pride is like putting your head under water, all sounds are muted and muffled. Get your head out of the water and you can suddenly hear what people are saying. Walk in humility with Jesus and your ability to hear Him will increase. Then your words will more likely come from a pure stream. This is a guarantee you can count on.

I think it is important that we always ask the Lord for his heart on a subject. We need to know how he feels about pride and the damage it can cause us. Let's look at what the Bible says about pride and humility:

> *Philippians 2:3 "Do nothing out of selfish ambition or vain conceit. Rather, in humility value others above yourselves."*

> *Proverbs 8:13 "To fear the LORD is to hate evil; I hate pride and arrogance, evil behavior and perverse speech."*

> *Proverbs 16:5 "The LORD detests all the proud of heart. Be sure of this: They will not go unpunished."*

> *Mark 9:35 "Sitting down, Jesus called the Twelve and said, 'Anyone who wants to be first must be the very last, and the servant of all.'"*

> *Proverbs 29:23 "Pride brings a person low, but the lowly in spirit gain honor."*

I would rather walk in humility any day then walk in pride. Yet because pride is so subtle at times, I find the best thing to do is have a heart check with the Lord before beginning each day and as I go to bed each night. You can easily do the same. Simply ask the Lord at the beginning of the day to lead and guide your words and to keep your heart pure from pride or anything else that would offend. Likewise, at the close of the day ask Him again, *"Jesus, is there any place in my heart that I gave to sin today? Reveal what that sin is, Lord, that I may be aware so as not to stumble again. Show me, Lord, if there is anyone I need to ask forgiveness of."*

I love our Lord. He is so faithful to help us. We are already forgiven by the blood of Jesus even before we ask it. We are made righteous in His sight when we give our lives to Him. Yet, in order to grow closer to the Lord as a person, we must learn to be okay with allowing Him to lead us into any area we need to repent. Remember to repent simply means to think like Christ in a matter instead of thinking in your flesh.

So many believers are confused when it comes to the topic of repentance. Some say, *"Once saved, always saved."* Others say, *"You must work out your salvation with fear and trembling."* My friends, both statements are correct because their essence comes from scripture. I want to leave you with these thoughts on repentance. Don't be afraid of it. Don't be legalistic with it. It is the job of every believer to repent when they realize they are thinking incorrectly. When you realize your thinking is not productive or beneficial to your life, simply repent, in Jesus' name. Change your thinking, change your words and you will change your life.

A person once said to me, *"There is no way you can be hearing God like you say you are. How come I am not hearing God or getting any visions. Why would God tell you stuff that He would not tell me?"*

My answer was and still is, *"God is talking to you all the time."*

Our God is a communicator. As you get to know Him and how He speaks, you will recognize His voice. He is not limited like we are. He speaks in numbers, words we see or hear, or through nature and miracles. He speaks through other people. God speaks through music or in a scene of a movie. God speaks to you in a still small voice like He did to Elijah. But the real questions are: *"Are you listening? Is there anything blocking your hearing? Is there anything in your life standing in the way of you receiving the words that God wants you to hear?"*

Let's do what the Word tells us:

> *Hebrews 12:1-2 "Therefore, since we are surrounded by such a great cloud of witnesses, let us throw off everything that hinders and the sin that so easily entangles. And let us run with perseverance the race marked out for us, fixing our eyes on Jesus, the pioneer and perfecter of faith. For the joy set before him he endured the cross, scorning its shame, and sat down at the right hand of the throne of God."*

Activation Prayer:

Heavenly Father, please remove anything that would hinder my hearing Your voice or seeing what You want to show me. Reveal any pride I may not be aware of that may be hindering my relationships with others. Thank You for the new thoughts that I can receive from You today. I give You every old negative thought. In Jesus' name. Amen.

Chapter Nine
EMOTIONAL WOUNDS

Pain

Pain is not something we experience only physically, but emotionally as well. I believe Jesus Himself felt all the range of emotions that we do. There are several scriptures depicting this.

> *Hebrews 4:15 "For we do not have a high priest who is unable to empathize with our weaknesses, but we have one who has been tempted in every way, just as we are—yet he did not sin."*
>
> *John 11:35 "Jesus wept."*

Matthew 23:27 "Jerusalem, Jerusalem, you who kill the prophets and stone those sent to you, how often I have longed to gather your children together, as a hen gathers her chicks under her wings, and you were not willing."

Mark 14:33 "He took Peter, James and John along with him, and he began to be deeply distressed and troubled."

Psalm 43:18 "The Lord is close to the brokenhearted and saves those who are crushed in spirit."

Physical pain is obvious and can rarely be ignored. If you were to step on a nail with your bare foot, do you think it would hurt? Yes, indeed. After you realize what happened, what will you do? Most likely you will take the nail out, clean the wound with soapy water or some type of disinfectant, put medication on it, bandage it and possibly go to a medical clinic to get a tetanus shot. But what happens when your heart is wounded? Often, people just put their chin up and fall back into coping mechanisms to ignore the pain of their wounded hearts.

It is so important to teach your children from the time they are young to communicate their feelings in a healthy way. Not by screaming and shouting or hitting and biting but using words or pictures to state how they feel. This is one of the reasons that I am saddened when I hear parents telling their children, *"Stop crying this instant."*

Consider instead working with your child. Teach them to communicate what is going on with their bodies or emotions. I am sure you've heard well-meaning parents say to their children *"Big boys/girls don't cry."* These boys and girls will one day grow up to be men and women, who have learned to stuff their emotions and pain rather than feel the shame of expressing them. Lately the saying I hear most often is, *"Put your big girl pants on."* Sometimes this can be funny, but in the long term if the pain is there, it needs to be tended to, just like a cut or stepping on a dirty nail.

I have ministered to many men and women who said it was not okay in their family to express their feelings, especially if tears or anger were involved. This leads to adults who have childhood wounds that have never even begun to heal. Because of this, these people don't understand why they react to situations with intense emotions. These adults often feel like something is wrong with them. Again, often the caregivers taught them not to bring up their pain and so they are still holding it all in. These emotions can pile up, something like emotional constipation. Jesus wants to heal your heart and remove the pain.

Sharing a place of pain is not the same as speaking a word curse or negative confession. I know folks that are afraid to say out loud that they have cold symptoms because they are making a negative confession. Please understand there is a beautiful balance here with our words. When Jesus ministered healing, He often would ask, *"What do you want me to do?"* Jesus wants to hear our needs so He can respond and heal us.

> *Mark 10:51 "'What do you want me to do for you?' Jesus asked him. The blind man said, 'Rabbi, I want to see.'"*

> *Matthew 7:7 "Ask and it will be given to you; seek and you will find; knock and the door will be opened to you."*

Have you ever felt defensive when your spouse or friend tried to point out a potential problem in your life or circumstances? Maybe you have even yelled at a person who simply asked you a question that was neither negative nor damaging, but at that moment you felt emotionally vulnerable? You felt sure the person was speaking against you.

What if this person accidentally bumped into a bruise from your past? What if the pain you felt in that moment was not even from that person, but originated from an unhealed wound? If you find yourself jumping to conclusions and releasing blame, you may have been wounded long before that person bumped your bruise. You just never knew how to deal with the trauma or the pain.

We will often use our coping skills that God gave us for our survival in the moment, which is good to do. However, later introspection and reflection are a lifeline to understanding why we were hurt and to free ourselves from the pain. There are times when coping is all we have at the moment. But remember, one day our emotions will speak at an inconvenient time, sometimes with a sudden panic attack or symptoms of illness because the pain has been stuffed so long that the body begins to erode in certain places. These unhealed wounds will have triggers with emotional reactions.

> Proverbs 17:22 "A cheerful heart is good medicine, but a crushed spirit dries up the bones."

This is one of the reasons I do healing the heart ministry with people. I like to see all lies exposed and removed. Then God's truth can be brought in to set the person free. I want to see people healed in mind and body. I want them to have a happy heart and a healthy body. Jesus does not leave us in these places of pain and wounding. He longs to have us come to Him for total restoration and emotional healing. This is the good news.

Shame

Shame is a tool of the enemy to lock your heart in a prison of self-condemnation. The enemy does not fight fair, never has, and never will. It is a good thing to feel badly for what you have done that brought harm to yourself or another person. It is healthy and can lead to repentance and restoration, which is a good thing. Part of our growth along this journey called life is in understanding that we need to change our thinking and our actions. But the shame used by the enemy is a stronghold that does not want to let go of its captive.

Shame usually begins to take root in our lives during early childhood years. Back in the day, it was not uncommon for a child to be disciplined by their parents and the words used were, *"Shame on you."* Little did the parents know these words were releasing lies into the very core of the child and their identity. The enemy takes advantage of our ignorance. Like I said, he does not fight fair. It's no wonder that so many of us struggle throughout life with shame. Shame can paralyze you and leave you feeling helpless and stuck, like a bug on a spider's web.

Shame is defined as, *"A painful feeling of humiliation or distress caused by the consciousness of wrong or foolish behavior."* [1] I experienced a lot of shame after rededicating my life to Jesus. I knew that his blood had set me free and that I was forgiven, but this voice of condemnation would get stuck in my head. I would rehearse in my mind bad things that others had done to me. The actions I took as a result, would leave me feeling so dirty and shameful. I would try to go to sleep and suddenly awaken with a foreboding sensation of shame and a memory of my sinful actions before rededicating my life to Christ. I would ask forgiveness again and again but still this oppressive battle would continue.

What I did not yet understand was the power of grace. I intellectually knew I was forgiven by Jesus. I knew by faith I was a new creature in Christ, that the old has passed away; behold all things were new (see 2 Corinthians 5:17). But why could I not feel free? Indeed, I needed a deliverance, not from sin habits as some would think, but from an oppressive demonic spirit of shame. People, I tell you this battle in my mind lasted at least ten years. That's ten years of wasted energy. That's ten years of being robbed of peace that Jesus paid the price for me to walk in.

Because of my own struggle with shame, I have compassion for anyone who is struggling in this area. So often this is a cycle that perpetuates the very thing you need freedom from. For example, let's say you have a weight problem. You start a diet, and then cannot resist the forbidden food, like a large slice of double fudge chocolate cake. You take one bite and it is so good. Then you take another and another. Before you know it, you have eaten the whole thing. Later you are left with the feeling of failure which leads to guilt, which leads to condemnation which leads to shame. At this point, most of us say to ourselves, *"What's the use? I just cannot lose weight, why even try?"* This cycle continues on and on and on year after year. It affects our self-worth deep down, even though we put on that happy coping face.

Very few stop and think that maybe they have an adversary, the devil, who does not want them to succeed. We should hit pause and ask ourselves a few questions when we see a negative cycle of any kind happening in our lives. A cycle is a clue to a stronghold; something we have touched on previously in this book. Some questions to ask yourself are:

> What does the Word of God say about this?
>
> What is God's heart towards me?
>
> What is the enemy so afraid of that he would try and stop me from reaching my goals or my freedom?

I can promise you this, the enemy is afraid of you and afraid of you reaching your destiny in Christ. If he cannot take your belief in Christ, he will do whatever he can to leave you feeling defeated. Joyce Meyers wrote an excellent book called *Battlefield of the Mind*. I recommend this book to anyone, believers and unbelievers alike. After reading this book I believe you will gain insight into the fact that you are not losing your mind. You have an adversary, the devil, who works on your flesh, which wars against your soul. God has given you the tools to overcome this adversary and you CAN take captive every thought in Jesus' name (see 1 Corinthians 10:3-5).

Activation Step:

Ask Jesus to heal your wounded heart. Ask Jesus to show you where shame entered the picture of your life and ask Him to remove it from you in His amazing name. Ask Him to renew your mind and reset your thinking as He gives you a revelation of grace and the fact that you are cleansed and set free by His blood. Then give Him praise and thank Him for your healing and deliverance.

Heartache

> John 16:33 (Jesus speaking) "I have told you these things, so that in me you may have peace. In this world you will have trouble. But take heart! I have overcome the world."

One could not possibly live this life without experiencing the pain of a broken heart. A heart ache is similar in the emotions as a toothache is to the body. You cannot eat, sleep or drink when you have a bad toothache. It is the same with a broken heart. Heartache is a pain felt deeper than almost any other wound. I have found that heartaches usually come with betrayal or loss.

Many songs have been written about this subject. Books have been written and poems penned. Chances are there's a song floating around in your thoughts right now. We all know what it feels like to lose someone close to us. Sometimes our first heartache came as children when a beloved pet passed away or in the sadness you felt when your parents fought, separated or divorced. God has something to say about this subject in the Bible. Here are a few of his thoughts:

> *Psalm 34:17-20 "The righteous cry out, and the Lord hears them; he delivers them from all their troubles. The Lord is close to the brokenhearted and saves those who are crushed in spirit. The righteous person may have many troubles but the Lord delivers him from them all; he protects all his bones, not one of them will be broken."*

> *Revelation 21:4 "And God shall wipe away all tears from their eyes; and there shall be no more death, neither sorrow, nor crying, neither shall there be any more pain: for the former things are passed away."*

> *Psalm 147:3 "He heals the brokenhearted and binds up their wounds."*

> *Nahum 1:7 "The Lord is good, a refuge in times of trouble. He cares for those who trust in him..."*

Imagine the heartache felt by a mother who opens the door to her home, only to see a police officer standing there to inform her that her child has been in an accident. Imagine the agony mixed with fear as you wait for the officer's report. This happened to my husband's mother when he was just five years old. My husband vividly remembers watching his mother talking to the police officer who came bearing the news that her seventeen-year-old son had been killed in an automobile accident. That little five-year-old boy watched as his mother collapsed from shock and emotional pain. This type of emotional trauma impacts an entire family. Loss and heartache can overwhelm your soul.

How does healing come after loss or trauma? Jesus will take you by the hand and step by step bring you into full healing. Regardless of the cause of your heartache, He is faithful. His Word promises that He has got you. He is with you through the storms of life. He says, *"Peace be still"* to the storm and it calms.

Remember Job? He was a righteous man, but a very jealous enemy, Satan, began to move against Job. Job went through unimaginable loss all in one day. If all that was not enough, Satan then began to torment Job with physical afflictions. It was during his physical suffering that Job wished he had never been born.

I believe Job to be a beacon of hope to all who are going through hardships that do not make sense. It was Satan that did all these horrible things to Job and his wife, but it was God who restored him. He not only restored what was taken but doubled what was taken.[2] You get double for your trouble. That is the kind of God we serve. He will do as His Word says and will bind up the broken hearted. He will restore and revive.

The Word of God is powerful. Get to know it. Memorize it. Speak the Word out loud over yourself daily. Write the Word on index cards and stick them all over your house. Remind yourself and God of what is written. The enemy will hear it too as you speak the Word of God out loud over your circumstances. This is a lifestyle. This is how I live. I could not make it without the Word of God in my mouth and a song of praise in my heart. The day to day tests come, but I can say with full confidence, the disappointments are all made small when you look to Jesus. Sing this song again and let His love wash over you.

> *"Turn your eyes upon Jesus, look full in his wonderful face, and the things of the earth, will grow strangely dim, in the light of his glory and grace."* [3]

Rejection often comes with heartache. My mom and three siblings had just moved to a new city when I was a freshman in high school. Everything was new and I was desperate to make new friends. I felt very alone and vulnerable. I met a cute boy who liked me, and I liked him. In high school, this was wonderful. He was a couple grades ahead of me and I was in love. This guy was in my thoughts, day and night. I would practice writing his name with mine, drawing hearts all around our names.

We had been dating for about three months when it happened. The betrayal. I had stayed the night with friends, and we had been partying. In this high school, the word partying usually meant drinking beer and sometimes smoking pot. About three in the morning, I decided to call it a night and found a couch to sleep on. When I woke up, I found my boyfriend in bed with my best girlfriend. My heart was racing. I wanted to yell, run, and throw something all at the same time. *How could this happen? How could she? How could he?* I thought I was going to die of shock and trauma.

The pain in my heart was so real, and with it came betrayal and a deep sense of rejection. This event would hide quietly in my subconscious affecting my day to day life in a way I was not aware of. What I did not know then is, I already had the pain of rejection, betrayal and abandonment in my soul from my early years of childhood when my mom and dad got a divorce. As often happens with these wounds that are left unhealed, I became a magnet for more negative experiences that reinforced the lie from the first trauma.

If you or someone you know is experiencing a heartache, please love them. Pray the peace of Jesus over them. Ask the Holy Spirit what truth He would like to speak to them. Ask what lies the enemy is trying to plant and get those lies removed. Always replace every lie with the truth. That's what happened with Job. He was regretting his birth.

He regretted his purpose and value and then God came and spoke truth to him.

> *Job 42:10-17 "The Lord restored the fortunes of Job when he prayed for his friends, and the Lord gave Job twice as much as he had before. Then all his brothers and sisters and all who had known him before came to him, and they ate bread with him in his house; and they consoled him and comforted him over all the [distressing] adversities that the Lord had brought on him. And each one gave him a piece of money, and each a ring of gold.*
>
> *And the Lord blessed the latter days of Job more than his beginning; for he had 14,000 sheep, 6,000 camels, 1,000 yoke of oxen, and 1,000 female donkeys. He had seven sons and three daughters. And he called the name of the first [daughter] Jemimah, and the name of the second Keziah, and the name of the third Keren-happuch. In all the land there were found no women so fair as the daughters of Job; and their father gave them an inheritance among their brothers. After this, Job lived 140 years, and saw his sons and his grandsons, four generations. So Job died, an old man and full of days."*

Memories

Trauma is defined in the New Oxford Dictionary of Psychology as "a physical injury or wound, or a powerful psychological shock that has damaging effects." [4] Whenever there has been an accident or injury, one of the first things the EMT will do after checking your breathing is to treat you for trauma. Usually they provide a warm blanket and wrap it around you, because when you go into shock, your core gets cold. The warmth is so important to keeping you alive. Literally, the word trauma comes from Greek origin meaning "wound." [5]

Two-year-old little Wayne sat eating his peanut butter and jelly sandwich out on the front porch on a blue skied summer day. As he did so, along came a large friendly dog. The dog decided that the peanut butter and jelly sandwich looked and smelled good. The dog took the sandwich from Wayne (with his teeth of course). Wayne began to cry and cry. For this two-year-old boy, the dog was big and mean and something to be frightened of. This was an emotional trauma for this two-year-old. After this event, any time Wayne saw a large dog, his adrenaline would rush through his body and all he felt was fear.

Physical trauma settles in different parts of your body, normally the part that was wounded. Emotional and physical trauma can be stored in your memory banks and can bring with it physical or emotional reactions years later. This is one of the reasons it is said if you get thrown off a horse, get back on. If you don't, chances are you will not ride again because of the memory of the trauma of being thrown.

When I was sixteen years old, I was in a pretty nasty auto accident. My friend was driving me to school, and we were running a little late. We approached a small intersection in a nearby neighborhood. My friend did not see the car coming on his right passenger side, because there was a large bushy tree blocking his view. We were hit. The car that hit us did not see us either because of the same bushy tree. On impact, I was knocked unconscious as my face hit the windshield and dashboard. I had not yet buckled my seat belt.

The good news is, all I suffered was a broken tooth, a cut to my face, and a few stitches. I wore a neck brace for a short while. I was going to be fine physically; however, emotionally I relived the trauma in my body every time I got into a car as a passenger. I would feel the memory whenever a driver would put on the brakes. Often, I would tense up and suck in my breath. I did not know then about the power of prayer through Jesus Christ who heals my body and my emotions. Jesus can remove trauma from your cellular memory. All you must do is ask.

When dealing with a traumatic memory, I find it is important to uncover any lies that the enemy may have attached to the event that caused the emotional or physical pain, or both. I then ask God, "What is the truth that You want me to know concerning the lie about the event?" I want to encourage you that the Holy Spirit is our counselor. He loves to bring healing to our souls.

> *John 16:7 "But very truly I tell you, it is for your good that I am going away. Unless I go away, the Advocate will not come to you; but if I go, I will send him to you."*

> *John 14:26 "But the Advocate, the Holy Spirit, whom the Father will send in my name, will teach you all things and will remind you of everything I have said to you."*

> *1 John 2:27 "As for you, the anointing you received from him remains in you, and you do not need anyone to teach you. But as his anointing teaches you about all things and as that anointing is real, not counterfeit—just as it has taught you, remain in him."*

> *John 16:13 "But when he, the Spirit of truth, comes, he will guide you into all the truth. He will not speak on his own; he will speak only what he hears, and he will tell you what is yet to come."*

> *Romans 8:26-27 "In the same way, the Spirit helps us in our weakness. We do not know what we ought to pray for, but the Spirit himself intercedes for us through wordless groans.*

*And he who searches our hearts knows the mind of the Spirit,
because the Spirit intercedes for God's people in accordance
with the will of God."*

While sitting at a church event, I was watching and listening to a guest
speaker as she put on a special production called *The Potter's Wheel*. I do
not recall most of her words, but I do remember she was sitting on a chair
on stage. In front of her was a lump of clay sitting on a potter's wheel. She
was giving an illustrated sermon as she formed the clay with her hands.
The room was dark with the spotlight on her as she wove her story using
scriptures.

It wasn't as much what the woman said, or was it? All I can tell you is that
the Holy Spirit began to heal my soul. Suddenly, I was back in time as I
saw my five-year-old self. I was crying and crying for my daddy. I saw my
daddy was leaving my mom and they were getting a divorce.

All I felt was pain, rejection, and abandonment. *How could Daddy leave
us?* At that moment, as tears were streaming down my face, I felt the
Holy Spirit bringing peace to my soul. As the peace came, I felt the Holy
Spirit speaking to me of forgiveness towards my father. *"Yes,"* I said, *"I
forgive my dad."*

The Lord took away the pain of the memory of that event. He did not
take the memory, but He took the pain of the memory. Does that make
sense? As peace washed over me, the tears continued, and my heart was
restored and healed.

Yielding was a key part in receiving the miracle healing of my heart. The
yielding was taking place inside of me. I had to yield in order to go where
the Holy Spirit was leading me.

Most of us have unhealed wounds. If you do, you will still hear the Lord
speak, but sometimes what you hear is filtered through your wound or

pain. You can only see part of what God wants to say to you because of this filter. Think of a mirror that is cracked and broken. When you investigate it, you can still see your face; but there is a distorted image. When you look in a mirror with no cracks or broken places, you have a full picture.

This is the benefit to a healed heart. The picture is clearer with each layer of healing you receive from the Lord. It is so helpful to discern what the Lord is saying from a healed perspective. Prophecy from a pure stream can flow easily from God's heart to yours, and from your heart to others'.

Activation Prayer:

Jesus, I thank You that You are my Healer. Not only do You heal my body, but You heal my soul. You heal the wounds in my heart. I give You permission to search my heart, mind, will and emotions. I ask You to reveal any place that needs to be healed. Is there a memory You want to heal? If so, reveal that memory. Jesus show me where you are in this memory. Jesus what did you want to do for me in that moment? Jesus, I give you permission to heal this place of wounding and I ask you to remove any trauma from this memory.

I ask You to reveal the lie that the enemy wanted me to believe when this painful event happened. What was the lie? I renounce that lie in Your name, Jesus. Now I ask You to reveal the truth that You want me to know. I receive this truth. Thank You, Lord, for revealing the lie, removing it and revealing the truth. I walk forward into that truth for my life. Thank You for healing my heart. In Jesus' name. Amen.

Chapter Ten

REGIONAL MUD

Cleanse the Land

Over time, I began to develop a passion for prayer. I noticed the more time I spent in prayer and waiting on the Lord, the easier it became to hear God's voice. I was developing the prophetic voice of God. I was a yielded vessel longing for more of God in my life. When I was able to, I would go to conferences and listen to some of the most respected voices on prayer and the prophetic. Some of these voices included, but are not limited to, Chuck Pierce, Cindy Jacobs and Rachael Hickson.

Learning from others is very important in your growth process. For me, sitting under these teachers helped me to grow in the prophetic and ignite my prayer life. These teachers inspired me.

I began to have a desire to pray not only for people to be healed and restored to God's original design, but to see cities and nations changed. I learned if you want to pray for a city or country, knowing the area's history can be valuable in uncovering the enemies' strategies for that region. I do not stop there. I can release the calling of that city and its people into their original, God-planned destiny.

In the same way that the Lord wants us to "see the gold" in people, He also desires that we would "see the gold" in an area. He wants us to begin to decree and declare God's intention for the area. Sharon Murphy authored a book on this subject titled '*Transforming the Land & Cities*'.[1] She received a similar instruction from the Holy Spirit and the Bible that I did. Sharon teaches you to pray for the land to be forgiven of known sins that have been committed on that land and bless the land back into its glorious purpose. When the land is healed, often the people living there are also healed.

> *2 Chronicles 7:14 "If my people, who are called by my name, will humble themselves and pray and seek my face and turn from their wicked ways, then I will hear from Heaven, and I will forgive their sin and will heal their land."*

We read in the story of Cain and Abel in Genesis 4:1-14. It's about the choice Cain had to resist the temptation to harm his brother.

> *Genesis 4:10 "The Lord said, 'What have you done? Listen! Your brother's blood cries out to me from the ground.'"*

Amazing. God heard Abel's blood cry out from the ground.[2] In Joshua 24:27, we read a similar statement about matter having memory of what has happened whether good or bad. *"See! He said to the people. This stone will be a witness against us. It has heard all the words the Lord has said to us. It will be a witness against you if you are untrue to God."*

This is why the land must be cleansed and forgiven. This is why we bless the land. The land carries the memory of the events that take place. I know this might sound far out there for some. No, this is not New Age. This is in the Bible.

Never did I feel this as strongly as I did while walking in Israel. My husband and I went to Israel in 2010 with Aglow International. During our stay there, we observed how creation was reflecting what God was doing through the wind, bumble bees, and flowers, etc. On one occasion while riding in the bus, we noted the beautiful sunflowers with their faces turned out as if they were smiling as we drove by.

The next day we boarded the bus and were told of a flotilla that was coming in to bring supplies to the Gaza strip, which could mean trouble for Israel. While we were there, the Government of Israel required all ships containing supplies from outside the port to stop to be searched. They wanted to make sure there were no weapons of any kind that could be used for war on the land. The flotilla refused to stop.

This meant Israeli soldiers had to fly out by helicopter and be lowered down with heavy duty ropes etc. There were injuries and accusations, along with further threats. This event was reported all over the news including in the U.S. As we drove away from our hotel, we began to pray. We were an army of intercessors; an army of prayer warriors for the land of Israel. We noticed the same field of sunflowers with their faces turned down. Every sunflower in unison had its face down instead of up as it had the day before. We knew that creation was responding and reflecting the conflict in the land.

> Romans 8:19 "For the creation waits in eager expectation for the children of God to be revealed."

Isaiah 55:12 "You will go out in joy and be led forth in peace; the mountains and hills will burst into song before you, and all the trees of the field will clap their hands."

People, the land needs to be healed. The land needs blessings and destiny spoken over it. When it is cleansed through the prayers of the saints and the blood of Jesus is released, we will begin to see God's goodness once again in the land.

There was a season of time that the Lord would send me out on secret prayer missions with a couple of friends who were also called to worship over and cleanse the land. We asked the Lord where He wanted us to go in our region of the Northwest. As He would give us specific instructions, we would travel from small towns to big cities. We went undercover on assignment to pray for the healing of the land.

Often, we would bring prophetic items that the Lord would place on our hearts, such as flags, banners or other specific things that related to the area we were praying over. After spending time worshiping the Lord, we would bless the land and release angels to come to the area. God even sent us overseas to do this very thing.

We then prayed for the church to arise in the area in unity as one voice to see God's goodness in their city. What an exciting journey it is to be a person of prayer, to learn to lean into God's voice and begin releasing God's purposes on the earth. Our desire in going out as a secret agent of prayer was to bring transformation to the land, spiritually and physically. We desired to see the areas known for depression to have an explosion of joy and peace. We prayed that areas known for violence and crime to be transformed into safe places for the people to dwell.

You can identify areas where the suicide rate is high. Pray and speak the Word over that area. Watch as the suicide rate drops significantly because life and purpose has been released into that city. When we bring transformational prayer to a city, how much more will the angels now be released where the people of God shine the light.

> *Isaiah 60:1-5 "Arise and shine for your light has come and the glory of the Lord has risen upon you. See thick darkness covers the earth, darkness the peoples, but the Lord arises on you..."*

Exposing the Enemy

As you become sharper and more experienced in operating in the gifts of the Spirit, you will be quicker to recognize and expose the enemy's activity. You can develop a stronger ability in the discernment of spirits. Let's look at a popular scripture regarding the gifts of the Spirit.

> *1 Corinthians 12:8-11 "To one there is given through the Spirit a message of wisdom, to another a message of knowledge by means of the same Spirit, to another faith by the same Spirit, to another gifts of healing by that one Spirit, to another miraculous powers, to another prophecy, to another distinguishing between spirits, to another speaking in different kinds of tongues, and to still another the interpretation of tongues. All these are the work of one and the same Spirit, and he distributes them to each one, just as he determines."*

Discernment means, *"the quality of being able to grasp and comprehend what is obscure: a skill in discerning, an act of perceiving or discerning something."*[3] When Paul was traveling through a city, there was a young woman who repeatedly called out "these men are servants of God."[4] Paul turned around and rebuked the spirit that was in her and it left her immediately (Paraphrased from Acts 16:16-34). You see, this young woman was a fortune teller and she had a spirit of divination, meaning she foretold the future through a demonic spirit. The enemy likes to be the source for information rather than people going to God for His Truth. We have people today who are under the influence of the spirit of divination. They are called mediums or fortunetellers.

> *Acts 16:16-18 "Once when we were going to the place of prayer, we were met by a female slave who had a spirit by which she predicted the future. She earned a great deal of money for her owners by fortune-telling. She followed Paul and the rest of us, shouting, 'These men are servants of the Most High God, who are telling you the way to be saved.' She kept this up for many days. Finally, Paul became so annoyed that he turned around and said to the spirit, 'In the name of Jesus Christ I command you to come out of her!' At that moment the spirit left her."*

I had an experience when I was first learning more about discerning of spirits over an area or region. While driving down a main highway, between cities, I was suddenly overcome by strong thoughts of doubt and unbelief that God was even real. These thoughts overwhelmed me. I began to have random thoughts, and questions like, *"Who is God anyway? Is he even real?"*

As I came out of the brain fog, suddenly I realized I was driving into a regional stronghold of doubt and unbelief. The demonic presence in that area was affecting the minds of those who lived there and was trying to impact me as I was driving through. *What?* The second I acknowledged out loud that these thoughts were not my own, but a demonic assault against my mind, the thoughts left and my mind became clear again. The fog lifted. This kind of battle, my friend, is more common than you know.

So often we take on negative thoughts as if they are our own. It is good to slow down and evaluate the situation for a moment. People have shared with me that they had thoughts about giving up on life or were suddenly burdened by lustful thoughts or committing adultery. The thoughts simply came upon them out of the blue. When they slowed down and took inventory, they asked, *"Where did this come from?"* They realized, *"This is not me."*

The Bible says to take captive every thought and make it obedient to Christ. Dark demonic thoughts will leave as quickly as they came when we do not own the negative thought, but rather take it captive. We must replace the negative thought with the truth of God's Word.

Back to my story. As I was driving through the area and was bombarded by thoughts of unbelief of who God is, I gained insight into the source. I then began to pray for the people in the area. I felt compassion for them. There was a lying spirit there who had set up camp and I was not okay with it. As I began to pray for the people that lived there, I was reminded of these scriptures:

> *Leviticus 26:8 "Five of you will chase a hundred, and a hundred of you will chase ten thousand, and your enemies will fall by the sword before you."*

> *Deuteronomy 32:30 "How could one man chase a thousand, or two put ten thousand to flight, unless their Rock had sold them, unless the Lord had given them up?"*

God is amazing at supernatural multiplication. Yes, that is the way of the Kingdom of God. Jesus also taught on the power of agreement.

> *Matthew 18:19-20 "Again, truly I tell you that if two of you on earth agree about anything they ask for, it will be done for them by my Father in Heaven. For where two or three gather in my name, there am I with them."*

I asked other intercessors to join me in prayer over this area where I had encountered this spirit of unbelief. The good news is, it didn't take long before the overwhelming oppression of unbelief was gone.

Activation Prayer:

Heavenly Father, we thank You for the power of the Word of God that it is living and active. We thank You for the power of the Holy Spirit that lives in each one of us. The Holy Spirit teaches us the source of our thoughts and how to war against the enemy over our minds. The Bible says we have the mind of Christ and we can take captive every stray thought. We thank You, Father. In Jesus' name. Amen.

Washing Your Feet

Many years ago, as a youth and prayer leader, I learned an important war strategy against the enemy and his attacks. I was doing a lot of one on one ministry. I had been meeting with a woman who was very troubled mentally and physically. I noticed during this time that I began to feel so tired and drained. I noticed my joy was gone. I felt depressed. I went to one of my pastors and explained how I was feeling and didn't know what to do.

The pastor asked me if I felt like I had been "slimed?"

"Yes," I replied. "That is exactly how I feel."

He simply prayed for God to wash off anything that had attached itself to me during the ministry time with this woman in particular. He also talked to me about having boundaries as a minister. He stated it is important you have taken care of you before you begin taking care of others. He called it fighting smart.

Years later, while on a mission's trip in a foreign country, I noticed a lot of sickness going on within the team as well as a lot of grumbling. We would go out during the day and see wonderful results with many salvations, healings or miracles. Yet the sickness and grumbling continued on the team. My husband and I felt we needed to ask everyone to take time for a heart check and ask forgiveness for any place they had been grumbly or fault finding. We asked Jesus to cleanse us as a group. The atmosphere did get better and sickness began to slowly disappear, but not completely. Some folks wanted to hang onto their seemingly justified offenses.

This is what I learned from that experience. When you are grumbling against your leadership as some were doing on this trip, you are not functioning in a pure stream. You will not hear a word from the Lord clearly as you need to. Your negative attitudes against your team or teammates can pollute the water of your words.

When we are going out to love on people, it is important to stay in unity. Even if you do not agree with your leadership, you must honor the position and do what you can to be a blessing as you serve the Lord. This will help you greatly as you minister.

I have one more story I would like to share from this same mission trip. On the last day, we were holding a giant crusade. The stadiums were full all over this nation, and our area was no different. People were coming from far and wide to hear the gospel message and to receive their healing. While we were on the grounds, a woman was begging for money. I gave her what I had, which was a protein bar. As she thanked me, she placed a butterfly hair clip in my hair.

Shortly after that, I began to get very sick. I rushed to the lady's bathroom with symptoms of the stomach flu. It was bad. When I was able, I left the bathroom. My husband walked me back out to the grounds. I suddenly heard the voice of the Lord say, "witchcraft" and I knew the butterfly needed to come off my head. In front of me stood a powerful woman of God, Bonnie Fishler. I asked her to take this witchcraft off my head. She did just that, in the name of Jesus. Instantly, the sickness left my body. The physical attack was really a spiritual attack. I needed to be cleansed from it!

Now, whenever I lead a team, I ask everyone to do a prophetic act for one another. Remember, a prophetic act is symbolic and can be powerful. I will have the ladies wipe down the other ladies symbolically to remove any thing unclean that may have tried to attach itself during the day and the men wipe down the men with prayer. We do this symbolically by simply brushing each other off, like you would clean dandruff off your jacket. This has proven to be an invaluable instruction, and wisdom from the Lord.

Wherever I go, whether to a nation overseas or my own backyard; if I have been ministering to anyone, I ask the Lord to cleanse me from anything unclean. If I am alone, I ask the Lord to send an angel to remove any "dirt or mud" that may have tried to cling to me.

In sharing this, I don't want to discourage you or make you afraid to pray for people without getting "slimed." That is not my point. Rather, go forth and do the work of the Lord. Minister as Christ has ministered to you, but just be wise about it.

This may seem confusing at first; however, understanding this principle will greatly help you as you go forth into places God sends you to minister. Let's look at what Jesus taught His disciples at the last supper.

John 13:1-17 "It was just before the Passover Festival. Jesus knew that the hour had come for him to leave this world and go to the Father. Having loved his own who were in the world, he loved them to the end.

The evening meal was in progress, and the devil had already prompted Judas, the son of Simon Iscariot, to betray Jesus. Jesus knew that the Father had put all things under his power, and that he had come from God and was returning to God; so he got up from the meal, took off his outer clothing, and wrapped a towel around his waist. After that, he poured water into a basin and began to wash his disciples' feet, drying them with the towel that was wrapped around him.

He came to Simon Peter, who said to him, 'Lord, are you going to wash my feet?'

Jesus replied, 'You do not realize now what I am doing, but later you will understand.'

'No,' said Peter, 'you shall never wash my feet.'

Jesus answered, 'Unless I wash you, you have no part with me.'

'Then, Lord,' Simon Peter replied, 'not just my feet but my hands and my head as well!'

Jesus answered, 'Those who have had a bath need only to wash their feet; their whole body is clean. And you are clean, though not every one of you.'

For he knew who was going to betray him, and that was why he said not everyone was clean.

PROPHESY FROM A PURE STREAM

When he had finished washing their feet, he put on his clothes and returned to his place.

'Do you understand what I have done for you?' he asked them.

'You call me 'Teacher' and 'Lord,' and rightly so, for that is what I am. Now that I, your Lord and Teacher, have washed your feet, you also should wash one another's feet. I have set you an example that you should do as I have done for you. Very truly I tell you, no servant is greater than his master, nor is a messenger greater than the one who sent him. Now that you know these things, you will be blessed if you do them.'"

Back in biblical times, most people wore sandals. It was common to have the owner of the home provide a basin of water for a guest to wash their feet from the accumulation of dirt and dust after a day of work or travel.

Jesus served His disciples and left an example for them to serve one another. Peter did not need a bath. Because he was a follower of Jesus Christ, he was clean. But his feet were not clean due to the places he had walked that day. There is a natural and spiritual implication here. Naturally your feet get dirty, but spiritually, they do as well.

Do you remember the scripture where Jesus taught about going out to bring the good news and minister to others? He gave these important instructions:

Matthew 10:14 "If anyone will not welcome you or listen to your words, leave that home or town and shake the dust off your feet."

I hope this helps you as you minister in prayer or counseling, or any other place you are sent. Just as you brush your teeth before bedtime, take a moment to spiritually cleanse yourself.

Activation Prayer:

Heavenly Father, I thank You for teaching me how to fight smart and how to be in this world and not of it. Thank You for teaching me how to be separate and yet very present. Thank You for the role model Jesus is for us in the scriptures. Jesus taught and demonstrated how we should live.

Father, as we go out about our day, may we stay connected to Your voice and allow You to guide and direct. Thank You for cleansing us each day as we pray. Each day as we ask You to remove any and all dust from our person. May we go forward, taking ground for You in wisdom and authority as You have instructed. In Jesus' name. Amen.

CONCLUSION

My hope for you, dear reader, is that this book has helped you understand the importance of receiving words or instructions from the Lord that are clear and clean, not muddied up with personal issues. Imagine being thirsty and picking up a glass of water to drink only to see particles of dirt floating in it. I know, like me, you would dump the dirty water out and ask for a new glass of water.

Prophecy from a pure stream is like mountain water flowing down from the source. It is clear, clean and refreshing. The keys in this book are foundational to hearing God clearly. The keys you have just read about, keys like worship and prayer, are the bread and butter of your walk with God. If you desire God to use you as His voice on planet earth, then it is important you develop in all these areas.

Choose to take the time away from all the noise and the clamor to rest at the feet our Lord. Learning from Him will give you the opportunity to develop your hearing heart. It will give you the nourishment you need to grow. There is joy in knowing that God is speaking to you. What He has to say is helpful not only for you but to share with others.

Remember, prophecy is knowing the heart of God on a matter. God will speak through His Word, a picture of something that has happened, something that is coming, or a forthtelling. Prophecy from a pure stream is about seeing others as He sees them, through His filter of love. Prophecy should bring encouragement. It will tell you that you matter, that others matter, and God sees and loves them all. Hearing from God will increase your faith that God is alive, and He is with you.

As we discussed in this book, there can be roadblocks or hindrances to hearing God clearly. Remember, we talked about the importance of forgiveness? If there is unforgiveness in your heart, you may hear the Word of the Lord, but it may be tainted with the dirt of unforgiveness. Like muddy water, it is no longer clear and clean. This is how we can miss it and 'hear in part and prophecy in part' [1] rather than hearing clearly.

To hear the voice of the Lord clearly in everyday life, it must be filtered through God's love. Not our human love with has limits and strings attached, but God's love. Remember, love is a key to a pure stream, and I believe one of the most important keys we have.

Take the time with Holy Spirit as your Teacher and Counselor, trusting that He will speak to you and show you places that need growth or cleaning. There is not one person alive on planet earth that does not need both. The wisest men and women I have ever met understand this principle. Just think about how wonderful it will feel to have any remaining roadblocks removed from your life and to move with His voice more freely and clearly.

It seems like a miracle that our God loves each one of us. He cares so much for us that He sends us the Word we need when we need it through the "voice" of His choice. His voice can come through a person, a scripture, a billboard, a song...and on it goes. I challenge each person reading this to run from religion straight into the arms of Jesus, allowing His Holy Spirit to teach us of His ways. The Holy Spirit reminds us that even the understanding of scriptures comes through

His help. Jesus told us the Holy Spirit would come and be our Teacher and Comforter.

Let us aim for that pure stream flowing from heaven to our hearts every day. Let us be open to be His instrument by which He speaks. Let us be known as those who "know" the Lord. Let us be known as a people that are not full of religion, because religion is full of judgments and pride. Rather, be known as those who walk in love before God and those God connects us to. Enjoy the journey to a pure stream.

ABOUT THE AUTHOR

Tina McCorkle came to know the Lord Jesus at the early age of three. The first time she heard the voice of the Lord was when Jesus spoke to her to give her life to Him. Tina gladly did. After a journey of joys and traumas throughout childhood, Tina knew the steady hand of the Lord. She married Steven McCorkle in 1983. They have four children and, so far, three grandchildren. They've served the Lord as missionaries, pastors, leaders and worship ministers.

Currently, Steven and Tina McCorkle are leading a ministry they founded together called 'First Fruits Revolution Ministries.' Their mission is to bring heaven to earth through passionate praise and worship. They train the Body of Christ to hear God's voice and raise them up to operate in the gifts of the Spirit. They raise up revivalists through a school they offer called 'The School of Transformation.' They have seen many people, young and old, throughout the world come to the saving knowledge of Jesus Christ and the victorious life He has for them.

*Jeremiah 29:11 "For I know the plans I have for you,"
declares the Lord, "plans to prosper you and not to harm
you, plans to give you hope and a future."*

Connect with Tina

For speaking engagements or
leading worship for your event or conference,
email: tina4kids@msn.com
TinaMcCorkle.com
Facebook @authorTinaMcCorkle

Connect with Steve and Tina

To learn more about Steve and Tina McCorkle's ministry go to:
firstfruitsrevolutionministries.com
or email: firstfruitsrevolution@gmail.com

ENDNOTES

Chapter 1

1. *Turn Your Eyes Upon Jesus* by Helen H. Lemmel 1922 Public Domain. www.hymnal.net
2. Luke 1:35 "The Holy Spirit will overshadow you…"
3. John 4:23
4. Luke 10:27

Chapter 2

1. Matthew 6:9-13
2. Acts 14:23
3. Daniel 6:1-28
4. Esther 1-10
5. James 4:7-10

Chapter 3

1. Hurnard, Hannah. *Hearing Heart*. Wheaton, Illinois. Tyndale House Publishers Inc, (1978,1986).

2. Hurnard, Hannah, *Hinds Feet on High Places*. Wheaton, Illinois. Tyndale House Publishers Inc., (1975).
3. Park, Andy. (SONG) *In the Secret* Performed by Andy Park, Mercy/Vineyard Publishing/Capital CMG Publishing, 1995.
4. Neese, Zac. (SONG) *The More I Seek You* Performed by Zack Neese, Gateway Create Publishing/CGM Publishing, 1999.
5. Psalm 51:10 (KJV)

Chapter 4

1. Grudge. www.urbandictionary.com/define.php?term=grudge
2. Psalm 55, Psalm 109
3. 1 Samuel 18:1, KJV

Chapter 5

1. Honor. https: www.dictionary.com/browse/honor
2. Silk, Danny. *Culture of Honor*. Shippensburg, PA. Destiny Image Publishers, (2009).

Chapter 6

1. Exodus 20:1-17
2. Roadblock. www.merriam-webster.com/dictionary/roadblock
3. 1 Samuel 8-31
4. Joiner, Rick. *Overcoming Witchcraft*. Charlotte, NC. Morning Star Publications (1996, 2001, pp. 24, 26-29).

Chapter 7

1. Ephesians 4:26
2. Luke 6:45

3. Sticks and stones.
   https://www.conservapedia.com/Sticks_and_Stones
4. Proverbs 23:7, KJV
5. IKEA. Bully A Plant: Say No To Bullying. https://youtu.be/
   Yx6UgfQreYY
6. G.E.M.S. Education. www.gemseducation.com
7. Masaru, EmotoLeaf, Dr. Caroline. www.drleaf.com
8. Matthew 21:18-22

Chapter 9

1. Shame. www.lexico.com/en/definition/shame
2. Job 42:10-17
3. *Turn Your Eyes Upon Jesus* by Helen H. Lemmel 1922 Public
   Domain. www.hymnal.net
4. Trauma. www.merrian-webster.com/dictionary/trauma
5. Wound. www.merrian-webster.com/dictionary/trauma

Chapter 10

1. Murphy, Sharon. *Transforming the Land & Cities*. Spokane, WA.
   Healing Rooms Ministries (2016). www.healingrooms.com
2. Genesis 4:1-14
3. Discernment. www.merriam-webster.com/dictionary/discernment
4. Acts 16:16-34

Conclusion

1. 1 Corinthians 13:9

RECOMMENDED READING

In this book I have very few actual works cited, but what I have is years of reading and learning through books that have helped mold me and instruct me. I add the recommended reading because I believe that these books could broaden your understanding too, thus further equipping you to be more effective in your walk with Christ.

Glory - Ruth Ward Heflin

Hearing Heart - Hannah Hurnard

Hinds Feet In High Places - Hannah Hurnard

Don't Hug a Grudge - Donna Perugini

Culture of Honor - Danny Silk

Overcoming Witchcraft - Rick Joiner

The Three Battlegrounds - Francis Frangipane

Armed & Dangerous Basic Training - Angela Greenig

Switch On your Brain - Dr. Caroline Leaf

Healing the Heart - Joan Hunter

Battlefield of the Mind - Joyce Meyer

Transforming the Land & Cities - Sharon Murphy

For further learning on how to get your heart healed or help others go to www.auroraworldwide.org Aurora Worldwide Ministries' Classes on Healing Your Heart

Made in the USA
Monee, IL
04 October 2020